DATE DUE

Punishment

THE U.S. BLOCKADE AGAINST CUBA

CRUEL & UNUSUAL
Punishment
THE U.S. BLOCKADE AGAINST CUBA
◆
MARY MURRAY

OCEAN

Published in association with the **Cuba Information Project**

Cover design by David Spratt
Cover photo by Osvaldo Salas

ISBN paper 1-875284-78-8

First edition, 1993

Published by Ocean Press
GPO Box 3279, Melbourne, Victoria, 3001, Australia

in association with the Cuba Information Project
121 West 27th Street, Suite 1202A, New York, NY 10001, USA

Distributed in the USA by The Talman Company,
131 Spring Street, Suite 201 E-N, New York, NY 10012, USA
Distributed in Britain and Europe by Central Books,
99 Wallis Road, London E9 5LN, Britain
Distributed in Southern Africa by Grassroots Books,
PO Box A267, Avondale, Harare, Zimbabwe
Distributed in Australia by Astam Books,
162-8 Parramatta Road, Stanmore, NSW 2048, Australia

Contents

Dedication

This book is written for the 101 Cuban children, cheated out of their full lives by dengue fever in the summer of 1981, and for Adelaide Bean, Jessie Cagan, Alice Glazer, Gene Glazer, George Harrison, Irving Kessler, and Cele Pollack who defend the rights of all children. It is also dedicated to the memory of Rep. Ted Weiss (D-NY), who worked to normalize United States-Cuba relations.

Acknowledgements

To Marc Frank, my partner and longtime friend, for his time, strength and support; Michéle Frank, for guiding me to the Caribbean; Gail Reed, for always pulling through; Leslie Cagan, for seeing the forest through the trees; Hilda Díaz, for helping others to make their dreams come true; Ivan Mora, for laying the paper trail; Michael Krinsky, for helping to explain it; Jo Anne Lawrence, for knowing how to get the job done; Carmen González, for sharing with me one of her most precious possessions; Heidi González, for caring for my peace of mind; Rosemari Mealy, for dropping everything at the last minute to help; Nancy Mikelsons, for finishing that one difficult sentence; David Deutschmann, for his blind faith and bottomless courage; and for his inspiring example, Dan Snow, who learned that Cuba's largemouth bass are jailbait under the "Trading with the Enemy" Act.

My deepest respect and gratitude is extended to Jane Franklin who has made all our lives easier by recording the history of U.S.-Cuba relations.

And last, I would like to acknowledge a corps of Havana-based journalists doing their part to pierce the U.S. information blockade of Cuba: Audrey St. John, Jorge Miyares, Ana Perault, Karen Wald, Langston Wright, Nury Acosta, Mario Manresa, Patria Ochoa, Carmen González, Thelma Rodríguez, Damián Rafael, Roberto García, Marta Martínez, Alina Cepero, Yolanda Fisher, Arnaldo Hutchinson, and Arnie Coro.

Mary Murray

Mary Murray lived and worked as a journalist in Cuba from 1984-1991. She presently writes on U.S.-Cuba issues for both the Cuban press and the U.S. media and contributes to "Cuba in Focus," a weekly feature on New York's WBAI Pacifica Radio. An interview she conducted with Cuban Foreign Minister Ricardo Alarcón — *Cuba and the United States* — was published in August 1992. She also helps coordinate the work of the Cuba Information Project.

Cuba Information Project

The Cuba Information Project believes that it is time to normalize diplomatic relations with Cuba, allow free trade and travel, close down the Pentagon's obsolete Naval Base on Guantánamo Bay, and treat Cuba as a neighbor. The Cuba Information Project is a resource center for efforts aimed at ending the Caribbean Cold War. For more information, to make donations, and to order resources, write: Cuba Information Project, 121 West 27th Street, Room 1202A, New York, NY 10001, USA. The coordinator of the Cuba Information Project is Leslie Cagan.

Foreword

"I want to know when the United States plans to start respecting international law and stop using the United Nations Charter as a club."

Miriam Thompson,
Executive Director
Center for Constitutional Rights
September 1992

This book is not many things: it is not the first to be written on the U.S. blockade against Cuba nor, unfortunately, will it be the last; it is not an account of life under the blockade nor of personal hardships or tragedies endured. For instance, I do not interview the mothers whose babies died from the dengue fever that spread when the blockade denied Cuba the means to stop it. This book does not describe just how Cuba has withstood Washington's wrath for over 30 years, how the island's industrial capacity grew 200 percent in the face of the blockade, nor the government's strategies that have kept its borders distinctly etched on the world map despite the tidal wave of international events that have threatened not once but twice to submerge the island.

What this book does provide is the political framework for understanding the blockade now disrupting the lives of a second generation of Cubans. The chronology (based primarily on the painstaking research of U.S. historian Jane Franklin) dispels many of the myths surrounding Washington's maintenance of sanctions against Cuba — myths that perhaps may have evaporated in other parts of the world but whose fires are still stoked in the United States to emit a smokescreen for an archaic policy. After having lost the cloud cover of the "Soviet menace," the "spread of revolution" in the Americas or Cuban soldiers in

Angola, Washington's Cold War policy against Cuba now hides behind criticisms of Havana's domestic policies. Still a distortion, this actually comes closer to the truth: the first U.S. sanctions against Cuba came as the revolution began to reclaim land under U.S. corporate control and hand the titles over to the landless. It was tightened as the island severed the century-old ties that bound it to the United States. While Washington may sometimes believe its own rhetoric, Cuba never has. In an interview in May 1992, Cuban Foreign Minister Ricardo Alarcón stressed that:

> At one time it was Angola. At another time it was Central America... But this is just the rhetoric. In fact, the only pre-condition that they have had since the very beginning remains the same: they simply do not like the Cuban Revolution. They never liked it and they have spent more than 30 years trying to recapture us. The diplomatic rhetoric changes according to the times but fundamentally Washington is seeking exactly the same goal: the elimination of the Cuban Revolution... But remember that it all began in 1959... when in May of that year we carried out the Agrarian Reform Law. Washington has never come to terms with that... The Cuba-U.S. conflict must be seen more in the history of our bilateral relations than in the context of East-West confrontation. That is why the discord continues even though the Cold War has ended and the Soviet Union no longer exists.[1]

In the minds of many, the blockade has always been on rocky grounds — morally, politically and legally. It not only flouts international law and accepted norms of conduct but the domestic laws of the United States as well. As written, U.S. law limits the use of commercial and trade embargoes to cases where the nation's security or economy is threatened. Regarding Cuba, the only national emergency ever cited as the basis for the embargo is the pending danger of communist aggression. You need only to look at a map to see who, by size and geography, threatens whom. But, even if you were to subscribe to the 1950 doctrine that world communism endangers U.S. frontiers, things have dramatically

---

[1] Mary Murray, *Cuba and the United States.*

changed in the last three years.

Going back in time, "The Trading with the Enemy Act"[2] was first written to boost the war effort in World War I. During the economic depression of the 1930s, the U.S. Congress extended the president's powers during peace time to enable the Oval Office to take emergency economic measures to avert a national catastrophe. It is telling that when President Kennedy first imposed the embargo against Cuba, the two countries officially retained peaceful relations. He was forced to rely upon a 1950 national emergency declaration issued by Truman during the Korean War, alleging communist designs on the free world — a notion so absurd that the U.S. Congress moved to erase it from the books in 1977. Neither then nor in the intervening years has any U.S. president declared any national emergency stemming from Cuban conduct or activities.

Updating the Act in 1977, the U.S. Congress again limited the president's emergency powers to times of war while writing new legislation to handle national emergencies during times of peace: the International Economic Emergency Powers Act [IEEPA]. Under that the president is restricted to imposing emergency economic measures only in response to an "unusual and extraordinary threat... to the national security, foreign policy, or economy of the United States, if the president declares a national emergency with respect to such threat." While this was supposed to govern embargos including the one against Cuba, Congress realized what a preposterous notion it would have been if the U.S. president was to declare a national emergency because of Cuba. So the Cuban embargo was given the honor of its own special category, exempted from the IEEPA and to remain under the auspices of the outdated Trading with the Enemy Act and in the "national interest." In addition, Congress admitted that in authorizing the president to maintain the embargo against Cuba, it was expressly acting to preserve "bargaining chips" for any future negotiations with Havana.[3] In other words, the embargo

---

[2] The embargo law found in 50 United States Code Appendix Section 5(b).

[3] *See,* for example, Subcommittee Hearings at pages 19, statement of Professor Loweneld; 103, 113, 119, statements of Assistant Treasury Secretary Bergsten; and 123 Congressional Record 22477 (1977), remarks

exists solely as a means of coercing Cuba into bending to U.S. interests, having absolutely no relation to protecting U.S. national security or its economy.

When the definitive history of the blockade is written, I am certain it will be easier to see Washington's policy as nothing less than the pressure politics of a large and powerful country, scheming (with the blind anger of a spurned lover) to once more possess a lost colony. A similar conclusion seems to have been reached by a delegation of U.S. veterans of the Spanish Civil War, World War II, Korea, Vietnam, the Bay of Pigs and the Cuban Missile Crisis who visited Cuba in June 1992. They returned from Cuba, calling on Washington to end the blockade:

> ...At the end of our fact-finding mission to Cuba, we have come to the following conclusions: Cuba is not a threat to the peace and security of the United States and that the Cuban people are suffering deeply from the unfair and inhuman burden of the present U.S. blockade. The Cuban conception of democracy is different from our own. It is, however, the inherent right of nations to define their own political systems consistent with their cultural traditions and history. Therefore, we urge our fellow veterans and citizens of the United States to demand that Congress defeat the Torricelli Bill [4] now and that the Bush Administration end the economic blockade of Cuba in all its aspects — communications, trade and travel...

As the blockade itself prevents a public airing of the issue inside the United States, you will find in this volume Cuba's testimony to the international community — its arguments and evidence that the embargo brandishes an extraterritorial edge and constitutes one of the worst human rights violations currently practiced by the country claiming to uphold the concepts of democracy and liberty.

It was in the spring of 1990, when the U.S. State Department — albeit a bit heady after the invasion of Panama and the Sandinista electoral defeat in Nicaragua — uncharacteristically laid its cards on the table by pointing to Cuba and bluntly

---

of Representative Whalen.

[4] See the chapter "Tracking the Torricelli Bill".

declaring, "Two down, one to go." As recently as August 1992, U.S. President George Bush hailed the embargo as a policy that has survived the passage of time. Thirty years later, Bush and other blockade supporters contend that punishment remains justified against the island for rejecting the "American way of life."

This work clearly makes no pretense of staying aloof from its subject. My stand is as clear as I hope are my intentions. Like the photographer who carefully frames and then shoots his or her subject, I too scanned and selected material to specifically expose the U.S. embargo against Cuba as a blockade that is meant to starve a people into submission.

Thousands of citizens from across the United States plan to boldly challenge the legality of their government's trade embargo against Cuba in November 1992. Asserting that they respond to a "higher law," the Minnesota-based Pastors for Peace will lead a "Friendshipment" caravan of 200 cars and trucks along 8 routes, stopping in 110 U.S. cities to collect bicycles, bibles, food and medicine to be brought into Mexico and then loaded onto a Cuban freighter. "This grassroots effort represents an alternative to the immoral policies of the Bush Administration," said Rev. Lucius Walker, Friendshipment organizer. For that reason, the pastors decided they would not apply for a government-issued humanitarian license to bring the relief across the border. "The embargo violates a number of international laws and treaties... Therefore, we feel that we are not only abiding by His law but by international law as well..."

I believe that there exist just two positions on the blockade: Either you oppose it or you don't. There are no grey areas, no half-measures to support, no safe middle ground. It is designed to retard Cuba's growth at the expense of the welfare and wishes of the Cuban people. No matter what the blockade apologists claim, trade bans against Cuban nickel or sugar, in the final equation, knowingly deplete the family food basket and cause shortages of medicines. Cuba is not a commodity-oriented society interested in providing a VCR for every living room. The hard currency its industries earn is recycled to spur on development.

Eight U.S. presidents have made no secret of the fact that the embargo is to catalyze a chain reaction in Cuba: trade sanctions are to spark economic decline, surging inflation and spreading shortages which, in turn, are to ignite social unrest; then, with a guiding hand from the north, Cuba is to return to the embrace of its northern Uncle. Or, as one plain-speaking U.S. Senator said: "Cuba shall become our 51st state." There may lie the heart of the contradiction — for both sides. The mainland, as the *New York Times* has said, is consumed by a perverse obsession with the independent archipelago while Cuba, argues Alarcón, will never settle for anything less than being treated as an equal.

> The day the United States is prepared to deal with Cuba on an equal footing, recognizing Cuba as a sovereign independent state, we can then discuss any legitimate... point of contention... There are bilateral problems that could be solved, but only if the two sides respect each other as equal partners... We would not ask the United States to change its government, social system, or its ideological foundations in order to resolve a bilateral problem...
>
> The United States would have to completely abandon any and all pretenses to determine Cuba's destiny. That would put our two countries on an equal footing. Accepting each other for what we are. Concretely that means that the United States would end the economic blockade against Cuba...

I have no doubt that the people of Cuba are resilient, having faced 30 years of adversity with intelligence and courage. While they have proven that they can cope, we must ask why they should be forced to continue to carry the burden of a U.S. policy that has no legal or moral backing? The global community must continue its campaign to end the blockade for it is economic blackmail that makes a mockery of international principles governing peaceful coexistence. In this vein, the Cuba Information Project and I offer this work.

Mary C. Murray
September 1992

"Hostile actions against Cuba, in particular the encroachment of its air space and territorial waters, and the reinforcement of the financial, credit and trade blockade and the persistence of illegal radio and television transmissions from abroad, which violate the 1982 Nairobi Convention and international law, should stop forthwith; the territory illegally occupied by the Guantánamo naval base should be returned, in compliance with Cuba's just demands. The Movement once again calls for the cessation of the economic, financial and trade blockade imposed on Cuba since 1961 and affirms Cuba's right to request the 46th session of the General Assembly to discuss this issue. The Movement renews its solidarity with Cuba in view of the persistence and intensification of these actions."

Movement of Nonaligned Countries
Ministerial Meeting held in Accra, Ghana
September 2-7, 1991

"No State may use or encourage the use of economic, political, or any other type of measures to coerce another state in order to obtain from it the subordination of the exercise of its sovereign rights or to secure from it advantages of any kind."

Charter, Article 16
Organization of American States
adopted 1948

"No State or group of States has the right to intervene, directly or indirectly, for any reason whatsoever, in the internal or external affairs of any other State. Consequently, armed intervention and all other form of interference or attempted threats against the personality of the State or against its political, economic and cultural elements, are in violation of international law. No State may use or encourage the use of economic, political or any other type of measures to coerce another State in order to obtain from it the subordination of the exercise of its sovereign rights and to secure from it advantages of any kind..."

Declaration of the United Nations
adopted 1970 without dissent

From trade to blockade

"They [the United States] are practically telling us that if we go ahead with the agrarian reform, they will strangle us economically... No country can have political independence if, when it issues a law, it is told it will starve to death."

Fidel Castro
October 1959

1959

January 1 July 26 Movement troops take key cities of Havana, Santa Clara and Santiago de Cuba. Dictator Fulgencio Batista and others from his government deplete the Cuban treasury and banking system before fleeing the island. At the time of the Revolution, the United States was Cuba's number one trading partner, accounting for some 71 percent of the island's total exports and 64 percent of its imports. U.S.-Cuba trade for 1958 surpassed $1 billion.

January 7 The United States recognizes the new Cuban government. Just two weeks later, international press reports circulate that Washington would consider imposing an economic embargo against Cuba if the new government were to enact policies counter to U.S. economic interests.

April Addressing the U.S. Senate Foreign Relations Committee, Fidel Castro asserts that healthy bilateral relations between two nations must be based on the principle of full equality — a point of view Cuban diplomats will reiterate over the next 30 years when in any negotiations with Washington.

June 3 Cuba's first Agrarian Reform Law goes into effect. Provided for in the country's 1940 constitution, large landholdings are distributed to 25,000 farm families. The measure is meant to essentially expropriate the 75 percent of all arable land owned by foreigners. Five U.S. sugar companies control more than two million acres. Washington rejects Cuba's compensation formula (20-year government bonds at 4.5 percent interest) and demands effective payment for the nationalized properties of the U.S. companies. Despite protests by the U.S. government and business interests, agrarian reform enjoys wide public support on the island.

June 5 A Florida Senator proposes an amendment to reduce the Cuban sugar quota. The Sugar Law is scheduled to be reviewed the following year. Soon after, the Cuban press publishes what is said to be a copy of an official U.S. document containing instructions for a trade ban on Cuba.

August 20 By Cuban government decree, the cost of electricity payments to a U.S. subsidiary are slashed 30 percent.

September and October Talk of an embargo continues building steam in Washington and the regional press. Cuban leader Fidel Castro charges that the measure is conceived as punishment for the island's agrarian reform.

1960

January-February Cuba nationalizes 70,000 acres of land under the control of U.S. companies, including 35,000 of the 270,000 acres owned by United Fruit. The United States protests the action and on January 29 U.S. President Dwight D. Eisenhower seeks the executive power to eliminate the Cuban sugar quota from the U.S. market. Brazil's offer to mediate the U.S.-Cuban conflict is turned down by the White House. On February 13, Cuba signs major trade agreement with the Soviets that is to include foodstuffs, machinery and crude oil. Two weeks later, Washington rejects a fresh offer made by Havana to negotiate.

March The U.S. government bans Cuban purchases of helicopters which the island wants for agricultural production.

April Cuba sets in motion plans to expropriate the remaining 200,000 acres of groves and forests in the hands of United Fruit.

May Cuba discovers a marked decrease in the number of U.S. freighters arriving to load exports for the U.S. market. Havana denounces this as a "subtle boycott" on the part of companies such as Ward Industries which had been sending on average one ship a month but, by May, has cut the trips by half.

June Foreign oil refineries, the sole facilities on the island, refuse to process crude that had arrived from the Soviet Union. During a news briefing, Fidel Castro charges that the U.S. State Department is behind what he calls an "unprecedented act of provocation" meant to leave Cuba without fuel. Twenty-four hours after the U.S. Congress begins debate on a new Sugar Act that provides the president with the powers to scrap the Cuban sugar quota, Havana orders the nationalization of the Esso, Texaco and Shell oil refineries. That mandate is carried out in 48-hours. The U.S. Congress some 48-hours later approves the revised Sugar Act. By the next day, Cuba passes its own law to nationalize all U.S. holdings on the island. One more day passes before Eisenhower cancels current and future sugar sales. Eisenhower says that his decision "amounts to economic sanctions against Cuba"; Castro assails it as "economic war."

August According to U.S. historian Jane Franklin, "the CIA begins steps to recruit members of organized crime for help in assassinating Prime Minister Castro." Providing evidence presented in 1975 to a special U.S. Senate Committee investigating the CIA, Franklin describes testimony from a CIA operations chief who admitted that his job was to "locate someone who could assassinate Castro."[5] At the same time, Cuba nationalizes all remaining U.S. factories and plantations on the island.

September 14-17 The U.S. State Department tells Fidel Castro that he will be barred from travelling beyond the island of Manhattan when there to address the United Nations. Cuba then restricts the U.S. ambassador in Havana to his residence over the same period of time. On September 17, U.S. banks in Cuba are nationalized.

September 30 Francis Tully, a U.S. State Department official releases a travel warning and advises U.S. citizens not to travel to Cuba. (This is the first shot in the U.S. visa war with Cuba which culminates in present-day policy of restricting most U.S. travel to the island.)

October 19 Eisenhower prohibits all exports to Cuba except for food, medicines and medical supplies. To export these items, all

---

[5] Franklin, Jane; *The Cuban Revolution and the United States: A Chronological History.* Ocean Press. Melbourne, Australia. pp. 31-32.

U.S. firms must apply for a special license from the U.S. Department of Commerce. Starting the next day, it becomes illegal to sell, transfer or lease any U.S. vessel to either the Cuban government or a Cuban national. Picking up on Nixon's language, the U.S. media describes the measures as a "quarantine" of Cuba. Canada announces that it will not honor the embargo.

October 24 Cuba responds by nationalizing all remaining U.S. holdings on the island.

1961

January 3 Washington breaks diplomatic relations with Havana one day after Cuba formally charges before the UN that the United States is planning an invasion of the country. The Cuban militia is on code-red alert.

January 17 Washington restricts travel by U.S. citizens to Cuba despite a 1958 U.S. Supreme Court ruling *(Rockwell Kent and Walter Briehl v. John Foster Dulles)* that "the right to travel" is protected under the constitution.

February 17 As tensions escalate, Brazil again offers to serve as mediator. In early March, the Kennedy administration rejects this second offer. On the eve of the Bay of Pigs invasion, Brazilian president Janio Quadros speaks of Cuba's right to self-determination and, for the third time, states his country's willingness to bring both sides to a negotiating table.

April 15 Bombing raids begin against Cuba as the prelude to the Bay of Pigs invasion. The United States denies any involvement while Cuba charges that the strafings are to lead to a large-scale attack.

April 17-19 An invasion force — organized, financed, armed and directed by the CIA (with the full knowledge of the Eisenhower and Kennedy administrations) — attacks Cuba on the sands of the Bay of Pigs. They are defeated within 72 hours. At the time of the invasion, U.S. firms are committed to some $70 million a year in trade with the island.

April 27 Cuba petitions the United States to enter into negotiations to end the hostilities and re-establish ties. The following day, President John F. Kennedy answers that communism in the Western hemisphere is "not negotiable."

1962

February 7 A total U.S. embargo against trade with Cuba goes into effect. In its shadow looms new legislation that proposes cuts in foreign aid to any U.S. ally assisting the Cuban government.

March 23 The U.S. embargo is again tightened, barring all third country imports which contain Cuban material.

September 8 NATO freezes Cuba's credit line but refuses to end relations with the island as Washington has demanded.

October 2 Trade embargo is extended to shipping — barring U.S. ships from touching Cuban imports or exports while foreign shipping firms that trade with Cuba are put on a U.S. government blacklist.

1963

February 6 Kennedy forbids any U.S. government-purchased imports to be transported on foreign vessels that stop in Cuban ports.

July 8 Embargo is again tightened, falling under the official "Trading with the Enemy Act" which bars U.S. citizens from engaging in unlicensed transactions with the island. Essentially thwarting all trade with Cuba, it also becomes a violation of the Act for a U.S. citizen to spend money for travel to or stay in Cuba. All Cuban assets on U.S. territory including over $30 million in U.S. banks are frozen (and remain as such today).

July 11-12 Washington calls on Britain, Canada, Mexico and Spain to begin economic boycott of Cuba by eliminating all commercial flights to the island. Canada's top Commerce official is the first to refuse, asserting Ottawa's policy to maintain ties with Cuba.

1964

January 7 Britain's minister of commerce affirms that British firms are free to conduct business with Cuba, that London has never boycotted the country and has no reason to start now. His statements come on the heels of U.S. State Department ire over an agreement by a British manufacturer to sell 450 public buses to Cuba.

February 18 U.S. shrinks aid to Britain, France, Morocco, Spain and Yugoslavia in retaliation for continued trade with Cuba.

May 14 U.S. questions Cuba's request to purchase some $15 million worth of medicines which Washington infers is an excessive amount.

August 3 Mexico asserts that it will maintain commercial dealings with Cuba in brave defiance of a decision by the Organization of American States to terminate trade and diplomatic relations with Cuba.

October 5-11 At the Egypt summit of the Nonaligned Nations Movement, a resolution is passed on Cuba's right to self-determination without U.S. interference.

December 21 Washington threatens to curtail aid to Spain if the country boosts trade with Cuba.

Over the next 27 years, the U.S. government maintains the policy of a complete trade ban on Cuba. At times the embargo is expanded: for instance in 1966, Washington prohibits the sale of food supplies to any country trading with Cuba; in 1980, the Republican Party's presidential choice, Ronald Reagan, toys with the idea of a U.S. naval blockade of Cuba in response to a Soviet troop deployment to Afghanistan.

A series of embargo-tightening measures during the Reagan years in office receive little publicity outside of Cuba. The most notorious example, cites Havana, occurs in the summer after Reagan takes office when a first-time epidemic of dengue fever erupts on the island, claiming 158 victims including 101 children. Cuba charges that the U.S. government bars a U.S. company from selling the island the pesticide Abate to exterminate the mosquitos carrying the deadly disease. Havana also says that the U.S. Treasury Department procrastinates on deciding whether Cuba can acquire U.S.-made fumigation sprinklers that Cuban health officials feel are essential to curtailing the epidemic. Havana eventually buys the goods in Panama and Asia but not after losing precious time and at higher prices.

The Reagan White House renews verbal sparring and offensive posturing towards Cuba. When in October 1981 two Cuban teachers are shot in a remote area of Nicaragua, the United States warns of Cuban "expansionism" in Latin America. Six months after taking office, the U.S. president only agrees to attend a conference with Third World leaders if given assurances that Fidel Castro — then chief of the Nonaligned Movement — is excluded from that summit.[6]   Other actions taken by the Reagan Administration include petitioning Moscow in 1981 to deny aid to Cuba;[7] increased enforcement of the travel ban against Cuba, accented by a Supreme Court decision that upholds the restriction because of the embargo;[8] new U.S. Treasury Department measures designed to thwart U.S. trade with third-country firms that Washington claims have links to Havana, and limiting the monetary ceiling on what Cuban Americans can send to relatives in Cuba; and enforcing a ban on U.S. steel and alloy imports from the French firm Creusot-Loire until the company signs a voucher promising that these products contain no Cuban nickel.[9]

It is worthwhile noting that Cuba has long considered its nickel industry one of the island's top development priorities, with possession of more than one-third of known world reserves — some 20 million tons. In the summer of 1992, the United Nations Development Program signed two accords with Havana to help exploit nickel and other minerals worth a combined peso-dollar investment of over 7.8 million. In 1991, Cuba exported some 60 percent of its nickel to the West and is pursuing a number of joint ventures in the field, including with the Canadian mining company Sherrit Gordon, designed to boost production shortfalls sparked by Cuba's current oil crunch.

EMBARGO BANKRUPTS SPANISH FIRM

A 1978 contract Cuba signed with the Spanish firm Piher Semiconductors came under U.S. scrutiny five years later. For a plant to manufacture integrated circuits and

---

[6] Castro agrees to stay away after consulting with conference host and Mexican leader, Lopez Portillo.

[7] This occurs when the new U.S. ambassador to the Soviet Union offers his credentials on October, 26, 1981. See: Franklin, *The Cuban Revolution and the United States*, p. 161.

[8] Regan v Wald, June 28, 1984.

9 Similar agreements are signed by Italy, Japan, the Netherlands, and former West Germany. After the Soviets made the same pledge in July 1990, Washington lifted the decade old ban on a variety of Soviet products that had once been manufactured with Cuban nickel.

semiconductors for radios and television, Cuba purchased machinery precision modules and equipment from Piher. The U.S. Consul in Barcelona accused Piher of violating the trade embargo by trading in U.S.-made semiconductors and high-tech. Denying this, Piher allowed U.S. officials to inspect the warehouses which stocked the equipment under dispute. The United States claims continued for two years, however, and went as far as accusing Piher of selling missiles to Cuba and blacklisting the company. The Madrid press reported that Spain's Ministry of Foreign Affairs "charges that the case represents the extraterritorial nature of the U.S. trade embargo." In the spring of 1985, the Reagan administration started litigation against Piher, asking a Washington court to fine the Spanish company $10 million. After Piher agreed to a $1 million out-of-court settlement, the company filed for bankruptcy two years later.

The administration of George Bush also picks up the anti-Cuba ball and runs with it. Despite a new law that aims to eliminate informational barriers between the United States and Cuba, just weeks after Bush takes office his State Department denies Ricardo Alarcón, then deputy foreign minister, a visa to attend an international conference at Johns Hopkins University. The president's son, Jeb Bush, is working for a Cuban American Republican who is an open admirer of Orlando Bosch, a terrorist responsible for at least 30 acts of violence, principally directed at Cuba.[10] Bush's Commerce Department tightens the travel ban for U.S. citizens authorized to visit the island and tries to prohibit ABC TV from broadcasting the 1991 Pan American Games in Cuba, erasing from the books another constitutional right — that of free speech. In April 1992, Bush stakes out international waters as the latest venue for his government's 30 year squabble with Cuba. The president, in July, asks the U.S. Senate to amend China's "most favoured nation" status on the condition that Beijing

---

[10] Jeb Bush was campaign manager for the first Cuban American elected to the U.S. Senate, Ileana Ros-Lehtinen, (R-FL).

significantly reduce its assistance to Havana.[11]

There are also mild warming trends in what many are calling Washington's Cold War with Cuba, most notably during the administration of Reagan's predecessor, Jimmy Carter. In 1977, for the first time in 17 years, U.S. citizens are free to travel the 90 miles of Florida Straits to Cuba. Carter spearheads other measures that lessen tensions: Interests Sections open in each country's capitals; the two nations pen an accord on fishing rights and maritime borders; the Senate Foreign Relations Committee is presented with a motion to end the embargo (which it ultimately rejects); and Carter cancels Pentagon war games at the U.S. base in Guantánamo, Cuba. This brief reprieve ends just 22 days after Reagan assumes office when a Cuban diplomat is expelled from Washington for allegedly promoting U.S. trade with Cuba in violation of the embargo.

The sanctions a decade later take on added dimensions. As Cuba watches its trade relations turned upside down with the dissolution of the Soviet Union and is stunned to see former Eastern European allies rallying around the U.S. flag, some U.S. special interests argue that the embargo today may be capable of accomplishing what it so dismally has failed in doing during eight consecutive White House administrations: by crippling the Cuban economy, bringing Havana to its knees.

In early February 1992, Representative Robert Torricelli [D-NJ] launches a new crusade against the Cuban economy and subsidiary trade with the island by putting forward legislation called the "Cuban Democracy Act of 1992." Torricelli designs a bill which proposes that U.S. policy toward Cuba should "seek a peaceful transition to democracy and a resumption of economic growth in Cuba through the careful and sophisticated application of sanctions directed at the Castro regime and support for the Cuban people." Torricelli claims it is the proverbial "carrot and the stick", but critics such as the Cuban American Committee Research and Education Fund complain that the stick far outweighs the carrot. According to Dr. Alicia Torres, the Committee's Executive Director,

---

[11] Contained in HR 2212, amendment #803, introduced by Florida Senator Robert Graham.

...restricting U.S. subsidiary trade with Cuba will be to deny the Cuban people access to much-needed foods and medicines because 70 percent of this subsidiary trade is in food and medicines. Representative Torricelli's denial of food and medicines to the Cuban people is nothing less than inhumane. Even in the embargo during the war against Iraq, the U.S. government allowed exemptions for food and medicine for humanitarian reasons... We understand that Congressman Torricelli has been heavily lobbied by an extreme sector of the Cuban American community. But most of the community is increasingly concerned for the well-being of their relatives on the island. This bill does nothing more than increase the suffering of Cubans on both sides of the straits of Florida.[12]

Apart from the Cuban American National Foundation, [13] which has a hand in drafting the legislation, the Torricelli Act garners minimal public support. A January 18 Miami *Herald* editorial describes the bill simply as "bad strategy":

The Torricelli proposal is a jumble of embargo-tightening measures that would punish countries that do business with Fidel Castro's government... it would harm U.S. relations with important trading partners such as Canada.

The bill rates similar bad reviews in *The New York Times* and even Torricelli's hometown paper, *The Bergen Record.* Cuban specialist Wayne Smith, the former chief of the U.S. Interests Section in Havana, dissects the bill as "mostly huff and puff," a return to a policy that has never worked:

The U.S. embargo up to now has been an economic failure. And

---

[12] Press Release issued by the Cuban American Committee Research and Education Fund on the night the legislation was introduced in the · House, February 5, 1992.

[13] CANF was founded in 1981 by wealthy exiles in Miami to oppose the Cuban government and influence U.S. policymakers and public opinion on issues such as maintaining the economic blockade of Cuba. Former CANF president, José Sorzano, headed the Latin American Affairs Bureau for the National Security Council during the Reagan Administration.

no wonder. It is not supported by any other country. [14]

Despite the opposition, HR 5323 is placed on a Congressional fast track and threatens to become law before the year is out. The legislation provides for direct assistance to "dissident organizations" in and out of Cuba. It seeks to dramatically increase penalties for any U.S. citizen guilty of "Trading with the Enemy," and will further limit the small numbers of U.S. professionals and writers currently authorized to travel to Cuba. The bill is complicated by several seemingly positive features, but there is little doubt that its passage would significantly heighten the tensions now plaguing the two neighbors.

Essentially, the bill's main aim is to further tighten the embargo against Cuba, including the placing of sanctions on third nations providing preferential trade with the island. This, many warn, is really an attempt to officially transform the embargo into a blockade. While none of Cuba's principal trade partners (Canada, Japan, Russia, Spain and Britain) do more than buy and sell through established market practices such as trade credits, the sanctions could injure developing countries which rely on U.S. aid and, at the same time, are attracted to the range of investment opportunities the Cuban market is now offering. For this reason and others, Latin American lawmakers condemned the bill while it was still in draft form. The following letter was one of a number sent to House Speaker Tom Foley from his counterparts in Chile, Argentina, Bolivia and Uruguay:

Esteemed Congressman Foley,
    As members of Parliament from Argentina, Bolivia, Chile and Uruguay and defenders of human rights, we want to express our preoccupation with the possible approval of the so-called "Cuban Democracy Act" legislative project under study in the Congress you preside over.
    This initiative of the Congressman from New Jersey, Mister Robert Torricelli, does nothing to ameliorate or solve the situation in Cuba. We believe that this new and total embargo will only bring new and bigger sufferings to the Cuban people.
    To introduce more conditions on the shipment of medicines would affect the right to life of those to whom it is

---

[14] *The Jersey Journal*, May 15, 1992. p.23.

purported to aid, just to mention one of the aspects of this legislative project.

The pretensions that by law the government of the United States can sanction those nations that trade with Cuba, violates the freedom of commerce and affects the right to self-determination and of non-intervention in the internal affairs of third countries, universally recognized as basic principles of international law.

That is why the signers of this letter, elected representatives of our own peoples, raise our voices to condemn this Torricelli initiative, in the conviction that we express the feeling of all those who struggle to see their love for freedom come to fruition

Juan Carlos Cafiero, Argentina
Carlos Raimundi, Argentina
Jaime Estevez, Chile
Hugo Carvajal, Bolivia
Rafael Michelini, Uruguay

Other regional voices such as that of Venezuela foreign minister, Humberto Calderon, warned that the bill is a throwback to the days of "isolationist policies." Ricardo Valero, head of the Foreign Relations Commission in the Mexican Chamber of Deputies, charged that the new blockade measures against Cuba "confirm the United States as the leading violator of international law" and are "detrimental to the sovereignty of other countries engaged in trade talks with the U.S." [15]

Torricelli's claim is that the bill will close existing loopholes in the embargo that allow U.S. subsidiary trade with the island. Smith and others counter that there are no loopholes since U.S. subsidiaries cannot be subject to both U.S. laws and the laws of the country from which they operate. Says Smith:

Just as foreign companies operating in the United States are required to comply with U.S. laws and trading practices, so must U.S. subsidiaries in, say, Canada, obey Canadian laws and practices. Washington's insistence that they comply with the U.S. trade embargo against Cuba was seen by the Canadian government as virtually a demand for extraterritoriality and as

---

[15] Mexican daily, *Uno Mas Uno,* April 22, 1992.

unacceptable. By 1975, the issue had become so heated that the Nixon administration decided it was causing us more problems than Castro; accordingly, the prohibition on subsidiary trade was lifted. Congressmen Torricelli and Guarini (another N.J. House member and bill co-sponsor) now wish to reimpose it. [16]

In a statement to the press in April 1991, as the Torricelli bill began winding its way up Capitol Hill, Canada lodges its latest objection:

> Canada has expressed its concern to the U.S. administration on sanctions on shipping as contained in the Torricelli Bill as unwarranted interference in other countries' commerce with Cuba. Canada joined the European Community and Sweden in a diplomatic démarche to the Department of State on 7 April, 1992 to protest the proposed shipping sanctions, and to encourage the U.S. administration to refrain from taking actions adversely affecting global shipping... Accordingly, Canada urges the United States not to adopt measures which could interfere with Canada's trade with Cuba. [17]

Reinforcing the Canadian position are individual parliamentarians, including Jim Henderson:

> If the Americans choose to trade or not to trade with Cuba, that's their business, and that can be respected, but the American Congress, the American government doesn't have any business telling a Canadian company or a French company or Spanish or Mexican companies or any other company in any other country in the world that they cannot do business with whomever they choose. I think that although Canada and the United States are neighbors and our people are to some degree cousins, being relatives doesn't give one the prerogative to direct their neighbor's policies.

The European Community delivers its own protest note to the U.S. State Department, requesting White House assistance in blocking the proposed law. The démarche reads in part:

---

[16] *The Jersey Journal*, May 15, 1992. p.23.

[17] See page 111 for the full protests issued by the European Community.

The European Community and its member States are seriously concerned about Section 6 of the bill which would have the effect of prohibiting U.S.-owned or controlled subsidiary companies domiciled outside the United States from trading with Cuba. As has been made clear to the Department of State on a number of occasions... the European Community and its Member States cannot accept the extraterritorial extension of U.S. jurisdiction as a matter of law and policy. In addition, the European Community and its Member States note with concern that the bill would introduce discriminatory tax penalties against U.S. companies with subsidiaries overseas which trade with Cuba, thereby providing a draconian economic disincentive against transactions which would be permitted in other jurisdictions. The bill, if adopted, would also prohibit any vessel from engaging in trade with the United States if the vessel has entered a port in Cuba during the preceding 180 days. Such a measure would be in conflict with long-standing rules on comity and international law, would injure international shipping and would adversely affect the European Community's trade with the United States. The European Community and its Member States consider that these collective provisions have the potential to cause grave and damaging effects to bilateral EC/U.S. trade relations. Furthermore, passage of these provisions would be totally inappropriate and inconsistent with the new climate of reinforced transatlantic cooperation. The European Community and its Member States request therefore that the Administration take measures to prevent the bill from passing into law... [18]

On the British front, Trade Secretary Peter Lilley also went on record, saying that what is Britain's, will stay Britain's:

It is for the British government, not the U.S. Congress, to determine the U.K.'s policy on trade with Cuba. We will not accept any attempt to superimpose U.S. law on U.K. companies. I hope the Congress will think long and hard before seeking to interfere with legitimate civil trade between this country and Cuba.

---

[18] *See* page 113 for full text.

That simple but strong message was sent to curtail presidential support for the other blockade initiative the brainchild of Rep. Connie Mack of Florida. The Mack Amendment takes deadly aim at U.S. subsidiaries operating in third countries, to abolish the allowance under U.S. law that recognizes subsidiary trade with the Cubans. When Lilley issues his warning, versions have already passed both Congressional chambers and the legislation is headed for the Oval Office. With Bush's signature, U.S. law will empower Treasury officials to confer or deny licenses on foreign subsidiaries — all of which is presently regarded to be outside the embargo's jurisdiction.

In its crudest interpretation, the Mack Amendment is a bold assertion that the United States believes it has the right to regulate world finance. The British and others view the Mack Amendment as an infringement on and challenge to their own laws governing trade. An official press release from London in September 1991 further explains the British position:

> Our policy is to encourage U.K. firms to exploit civil market opportunities in Cuba. Our exports to Cuba were worth 39 million pounds in 1990. U.K. imports from Cuba amounted to 30 million pounds. In addition, Cuban sugar futures are traded on the London Futures and Options Exchange (FOX). A number of FOX members have used U.S. parents. According to U.S. figures, the dollar value of licensed U.K. exports from the U.K. to Cuba was $17 million in 1990 and $884 million in the period 1980-90.

The press statement then informs Washington that no matter what legislative action may transpire on Capitol Hill, London will do whatever is necessary to protect its own investments. Already on the books is the 1980 law entitled "The Protection of Trading Interests Act", (PTIA), that instructs British chartered companies to simply ignore U.S. laws such as the Mack Amendment.

> The PTIA became law in 1980 to... provide a legal response to such extraterritorial measures. Under Section I, the Secretary of State may counter measures taken by or under the law of an overseas country for regulating or controlling international

trade. The Secretary of State can make an Order applying the Act to the overseas measures, either generally or with reference to particular cases. The precise wording of any Orders and Directions under the Act would be drafted immediately after the Mack Amendment is passed by the Congress but before it becomes law... Use of the Act would demonstrate the serious view that Her Majesty's Government takes of any action to superimpose foreign law on firms trading in the U.K.

In addition to Britain, 17 countries have similar laws to nullify the impact of any new U.S. subsidiary trade regulation whether it applies to their country's trade with Cuba or not. They include the Netherlands, France, Germany, Canada and Switzerland.

Value of trade (in millions of dollars) with Cuba from 1980-89, by location, of U.S. firms' subsidiaries:

United Kingdom	797.01
Canada	580.23
Switzerland	523.20
Argentina	214.72
Spain	78.23
France	56.68
Panama	55.50
Mexico	38.65
Brazil	32.11
Venezuela	17.13

U.S. Department of Treasury, Office of Foreign Assets Control

The overseas operations of a number of U.S. parent companies also jumped into the fray to oppose the legislation. A spokesperson for Cargill Inc, an international trading firm headquartered in both the United States and Switzerland, complained that, "the ramifications of the Mack Amendment are tremendous for Cargill." If Cargill is denied access to the Cuban market, European and Japanese traders "would be very happy to take up the slack." The loss for Cargill and others would be substantial. A U.S. Treasury Department report asserts that during the 1980s, U.S. subsidiaries engaged in some $2.7 billion in licensed trade with Cuba. The study notes that in 1988, the year before the upheaval in Eastern Europe, Cuba purchased some $56 million worth of "grain, wheat and other consumables" from U.S. subsidiaries. That figure grew to $114 million the next year and leaped to $500 million by 1990.

Cuba maintains that with or without the new legislation — by virtue of a superpower trade ban against a Third World country and the United States' commanding presence in the international market — the embargo was long ago converted into a blockade. In a letter to the Secretary-General of the United Nations, then Cuban Ambassador Ricardo Alarcón explains:

> The discriminatory measures against Cuba in the world of finance — the ban on the use of the United States dollar, the denial of access to the United States banking system and the boycott imposed on it in international financial and credit institutions — have been a major obstacle for Cuba's international economic — and especially commercial — relations, and have limited even more the possibilities of external financing of the Cuban economy. The United States Government has also tried to compel third countries to apply such a policy against Cuba, even seeking to impose its own discriminatory legislation beyond the confines of its national jurisdiction, thereby violating the sovereignty of other States. In its most recent legislative session, the United States Congress to that end adopted new measures which clearly are unlawful and violate international principles and norms... the decisive weight of the United States in the world economy and its renewed efforts to perpetuate and extend this policy have transformed the economic embargo into a serious obstacle for Cuba's independence and development, causing continuing material damage and harm to the Cuban people. [19]

As entitled by United Nations' procedure, Havana requested that the item "Necessity of ending the economic, commercial and financial embargo imposed by the United States of America against Cuba" be placed on the 1991 agenda of the General

---

[19] Letter dated August 16, 1991 from the Permanent Representative of Cuba to the United Nations addressed to the Secretary General of the United Nations. UN document #A/46/193.

Assembly. Ambassador Alarcón's plan was to contend that the embargo constitutes a violation of the human rights of the Cuban people, as defined in the Charter of the United Nations and the accepted international precept that every country retains its inalienable right to determine its own economic, social and political systems free of foreign interference. While Cuba had consistently raised the inhumanity of the U.S. embargo to different U.N. committees, this was to be the first time that the full weight of the 30-year blockade would be measured on a human rights scale.

> The United States embargo has caused Cuba substantial material losses and has obliged it to make extraordinary efforts to change its economic relations, which in the past were entirely dependent on the United States market. This has entailed intensive readaptation of the structure of production, consumption and services to different types of technology, equipment, raw materials and consumer goods from other countries, in many cases obtained at short notice, all of which has caused enormous economic and social damage and hardship... It should be emphasized that the embargo continues to include a total prohibition on Cuba's acquisition of foodstuffs, medicine and medical supplies and equipment of United States origin. This criminal practice, applied totally and systematically for three decades, has caused and still causes appreciable additional harm to the Cuban people... The United States embargo against Cuba constitutes a flagrant violation of the principles of sovereign equality of States and non-intervention in their internal affairs, and is a constant source of tension that impairs the normal development of international relations. [20]

Within seven days of the Cuban appeal, made on August 16, 1991, the U.S. Department of State circulated its official objection:

> The United States embargo of Cuba is not an appropriate issue for discussion at the United Nations. Every Government has a right and a responsibility to choose the Government with which it wishes to have commercial and political relations... Ambassador Alarcón is mistaken in calling the embargo a

---

20 Ibid.

blockade. A blockade implies that the United States is taking actions to prevent other countries from trading with Cuba. That is clearly not the case. [21]

Alarcón responded by releasing documentation to demonstrate the long arm of the U.S. embargo. The list of spoiled commercial transactions with third country firms include a sale by the Japanese company Toshiba of medical equipment used to detect cardiovascular diseases and blood analysis laboratory equipment from the Swedish firm LKB. The U.S. government also prohibited another Japanese firm, Nihon Kohden, from filling a Cuban order for a machine that detects neurological and ophthalmologic diseases. U.S. Commerce officials also forbade the Argentine supplier Medix from shipping spare parts needed by Cuban hospitals to maintain U.S.-made dialysis machines and ophthalmologic sonar equipment already in use throughout the island.[22]

Alarcón proceeded to summarize 12 areas which he asserted demonstrates the U.S. intention to extend the economic embargo against Cuba beyond U.S. borders. The most salient points of the U.S. Commerce Department's third country export prohibitions to Cuba include:

1. products that contain any U.S. component or material;
2. goods acquired by third country suppliers irrespective of whether the goods were originally obtained for the purpose of re-sale or how long the supplier has possessed the product;
3. products based on U.S. design or technology including products wholly manufactured in a third country and containing no U.S. components or materials;
4. subjecting third-country companies under the control of a U.S. corporation or financier to compliance with the trade ban including in cases where U.S. ownership interest is a minority

---

[21] Letter dated August 21, 1991 from the Department of State of the United States of America addressed to the Secretary General of the United Nations.

[22] See page 59 for more examples of Cuban trade agreements undermined by the U.S. blockade.

share;

5. prohibiting access by third-country companies with minority participation by Cuban nationals to financial or commercial dealings with the U.S. government or its nationals;

6. prohibiting third-country banks from maintaining U.S. dollar accounts for a Cuban corporation or national or using U.S. currency in transactions between third-country nationals and Cuban nationals;

7. bars the importation of goods produced in a third country and by a third-country firm which contains any component grown, produced or manufactured in Cuba. [23]

On September 18, 1991, Ambassador Alarcón presented his government's formal request to the 46th Session of the General Assembly to examine the need to "end the U.S. blockade against Cuba." At the same time, Alarcón issues a blistering accusation that Cuba's adversaries are trying to muffle debate:

> The Government of the United States wants to prevent a public discussion on the criminal blockade it has imposed on Cuba for more than 30 years. As stated by the State Department last August 21, the analysis of this item by the United Nations would be "inappropriate." If we were to believe the... American declaration, it would seem that Cuba... is seeking to damage the sovereignty of the United States — a poor country that has the right to make its own decision regarding with whom it wishes to have diplomatic or economic relations... Apparently, Cuba is the one threatening the self-determination of the United States and is even trying to mobilize the international community to exert illegitimate and arbitrary pressure [over Washington]... Furthermore, they claim that the request to introduce the item is out of the question since it is not a blockade but merely an embargo. They suggest that while the United States has no relations with Cuba, they do nothing to prevent others from having them. The statement... takes for granted... [that] the international community exists in a total state of ignorance concerning the facts.

---

[23] Official UN document #A/46/193/Add.7.

Alarcón continues with an outline of Cuba's position: Washington's trade ban violates the bilateral agreements that were in force between Cuba and the United States at the time the embargo was imposed; contravenes the General Agreement on Tariffs and Trade and subsequent GATT decisions; contradicts the basic principles of the UN Charter dictating international relations and ethical standards; and is the root cause of material hardship in Cuba. As such, advises Alarcón, the General Assembly should consider the question of the embargo as a human rights violation against the Cuban people and possibly even a violation of the rights of the people of the United States:

> That policy, among other things, totally prevents Cuba from purchasing medicines in the American market and also implies many other restrictions to communications and contacts between both countries which seriously affect all Cubans causing great sufferings to its people... The violation of the rights of citizens... by the blockade against Cuba... would deserve further discussion. I will only mention two examples. The poor in the United States also suffer from meningitis B but they are prevented from vaccination against it as, so far, the only vaccine is manufactured in Cuba and is banned from the American market. Mr. Dan Snow was condemned to 90 days imprisonment, 5 years probation and fined $5,000 because he participated in fishing activities in Cuban waters... for Washington, it is not enough to try to apply its law beyond its borders. It also exerts every kind of pressure and threats, and punishes foreign enterprises which, nevertheless, maintain commercial and economic ties with Cuba.

Alarcón asked that Cuba be allowed to present its case to the General Assembly, that the UN intervene on the side of international law and that the office of the secretary-general be responsible for implementing the UN mandate. The draft resolution called for

> ...Reaffirming the right of every country to freely choose its economic, commercial and financial partners, in exercise of its national sovereignty, without any constraint or interference,

1. Declares that the policy [the embargo] contradicts the principles embodied in the Charter of the United Nations and in international law;

2. Affirms the necessity of ending that policy and, to that effect, calls for an immediate end to the measures and actions comprising it;

3. Invites the international community to extend to Cuba the necessary cooperation to mitigate the consequences of that policy;

4. Requests the Secretary-General to report to the General Assembly at its 47th session on the implementation of the present resolution;

5. Decides to include the item... in the provisional agenda of the 47th session of the General Assembly.[24]

Alarcón circulated documentation illustrating numerous occasions in recent years when the U.S. Commerce Department blocked third-country trade purchases by Cuba. The shortest list included eye drops, truck tires, hydraulic components, "v" transmission belts, pre-packaged airline food, electrical controls and regulators, materials for electrical installation, electric accessories, heater components, wood-cutting tools, metal-cutting tools, iron connectors used in electrical installation, light bulbs, electrical fuses and switches, plastic and water-treatment resins, cellophane paper, material to produce telephone cables, filters, motor glue and soft drinks. Not strategic materials, Alarcón emphasized, but parts vital to a smoothly-run Cuban economy. Some purchases could be done without, he explained, but Cuba refuses to economize on imports needed to keep its medical system one of the most effective in a region plagued by cholera and other "Third World" diseases.

One document traces the embargo's 30-year effect on the health of the Cuban people, beginning with the braindrain to the United States of the island's medical personnel during the early years of Cuba's revolution and ending with examples of embargoed health-related items. The Cubans purposely left that list incomplete out of fear of tipping their hand to the U.S.

---

[24] A/46/L.20. November 11, 1991.

Commerce Department, as they say has happened before.

> Of the 6,300 doctors in Cuba, 50 percent left the country —
> seriously impeding services to the population as well as
> university instruction. More than 40,000 medical products were
> registered in the Cuban market in 1959 (including medicines,
> reagents, disposable materials, instruments, etc); more than 80
> percent of which were of foreign origin — principally from the
> United States... pharmaceutical companies began cutting back
> and eventually suspended supplies entirely.[25]

Even though Cuba sought supplies elsewhere, the paper
continues, the country continued to face roadblocks erected by U.S.
companies controlling the pharmaceutical and medical
technology markets.

> Cuba's National Health System is extensive... [yet] the
> economic embargo seriously affects medical costs as well as
> limits the use of medicines, reagents, medical equipment, non-
> medical equipment, types of technology and investments. This
> has repercussions upon medical care, hygiene and
> epidemiology, medical education, research, and medical
> investment: in short, all the components of the system are
> affected. [26]

The Cuban firm Medicuba, responsible for maintaining the
island's medical supplies, estimates that the country wastes $4
million to $5 million every year in procuring medical products
that could be transported from the United States for one-third of
the cost.

> ...Medicuba spends $6 million for medical air and sea freight
> alone. If the same products were obtained in nearer markets,
> transport costs would be only $1 million to $2 million.[27]

---

[25] "Adverse consequences of the economic embargo by the United
States of America upon the enjoyment of human rights by the Cuban
people." Prepared by Cuba's Ministry of Health, 1991.
[26] Ibid.
[27] Ibid.

Cuba also imports some $750,000 in U.S. medicines acquired on foreign markets for an additional 40 percent cost. The same applies to reagents and sophisticated medical equipment such as Gamma cameras, used for non-surgical detection of disease. Since the 1981 dengue fever epidemic, Cuba spends on average $1.5 million a year for insecticides. Over the last 10 years, $5 million of that (one-third) was absorbed by blockade-induced transport costs. In 1991, Cuba's medical-related purchases surpassed $150 million in convertible currency. The Cuban ministry of public health, MINSAP, believes that without the blockade, Cuba would see a 30 percent saving — some $45 million. [28]

Additional facts show why Havana believes that the blockade is designed to threaten the health of the Cuban people.

Almost all computerized equipment involves electronic components patented in the United States. This requires suppliers from other countries to solicit licenses from the United States government, requests routinely denied when the equipment is being sold to Cuba. When such equipment is actually obtained, we've experience long delays in delivery like in the case of Nuclear Magnetic Resonance equipment (used to diagnose pathologies which escape traditional x-ray). When replacement parts are needed, licenses must again be sought from the United States. All of this impedes delivery of services to patients. [29]

The Cuban ministry of public health has also been forced to sidestep the blockade on routine items such as rubber catheters, tubing and mini-R x-ray film [used to diminish radiation exposure in its national screening program for the early detection of breast cancer] to something called a chromatographic column, a piece of equipment medical researchers say is a must.

In October 1991, the UN General Assembly adopted Alarcón's petition to review the item, stamping it number 142. The United States accelerated its opposition to holding any discussion. It was

---

[28] Ibid.

[29] Ibid.

curious that while the U.S. Mission in New York would continue to stress that the subject was "inappropriate" for UN consideration, the State Department back in Washington would contend that the embargo falls within "international law." Officials, however, remained unwilling to prove that before the entire General Assembly. There were other contradictions in the U.S. logic. A démarche circulated to all UN member states on the one hand, accused Cuba of trying "to resurrect old superpower antagonisms at a time when a new spirit of international cooperation has taken root in the UN" while on the other, remarked that the embargo was a way to "limit the flow of hard currency which can be used by the Cuban government to support insurgency in El Salvador." Washington itself had not only unearthed the rhetoric of the Cold War but fell into its own trap by omitting the very important role the UN had played in ending that Central American conflict.

Blaming domestic Cuban policy for the "hardship and suffering" of the Cuban people, the State Department engaged in what Alarcón was to later describe as "the arm-twisting of the international community." The same document that Alarcón is certain went to governments around the world issued the not-too-veiled warning that:

> ...the Cubans should understand that their insistence that you support them threatens your good relationship with the United States.. In view of your relations with them, we would appreciate your going to the Cubans in an effort to have the resolution withdrawn.[30]

Cuba did ask the General Assembly to table the discussion but for an entirely different reason. By the time the item reached the floor on November 13, Cuba had lined up initial support from a number of countries anxious to condemn the 30-year trade blockade. On the scheduled speaker's list, only Panama had signed up to bolster the U.S. side. In Alarcón's opening remarks,

---

[30] The document was never formally submitted to the United Nations but was delivered to governments around the world by U.S. state department officials.

he again charged the United States with launching a "frantic and inordinate campaign of intimidation, threats and pressure" that hampered the freedom to speak without "fear of reprisal." On those grounds, he suggested that discussion on the draft resolution be postponed until the following year.

One African state that had been willing to risk U.S. disfavor wished to place the blockade in the context of the Third World and the principles that hang dangerously in the balance for the entire international community:

> This debate is not about the bilateral relations between Cuba and the United States of America. It is also not about the different political and economic systems which the two countries have embraced... It is about the right of countries, whatever their size, ideological persuasion or level of development, to chose, without interference from any quarter, their partners in international economic and commercial relations... the duty of states, big and small, rich and poor, to respect the Charter and international law governing the conduct of relations between states. It is about the duty of the... UN to secure compliance by all Member States with their obligations under the Charter and numerous resolutions of the General Assembly... The last two and one-half years have seen fundamental changes in the international arena... Many intractable conflicts have found solutions in which bitter enemies have become reconciled and old rivalries buried. Sadly, the 30-year-old dispute between the USA and Cuba has remained one of the few exceptions not to benefit from the new climate of reconciliation, dialogue and accommodation. This is tragic... By accepting Cuba as an equal member of the region, the countries of Latin America and the Caribbean region have proclaimed as loudly as they can that Cuba poses no threat to anyone. They have also conceded to Cuba the right to organize its affairs in accordance with the wishes of the people of Cuba. We in this Assembly should call on all countries in this hemisphere to follow that example." [31]

---

[31] Information gathered from a protected source.

In other words, if Latin America can accept the reality of a socialist Cuba as a neighbor, why can't the United States.

In his formal presentation of November 13, 1991 Alarcón pressed the question of a human rights violation. Waving before the General Assembly a list of medical supplies which doctors at Havana's pediatric cardiac hospital had trouble purchasing last year, Alarcón asserted:

> I do not intend to read this document... but the least I can do is mention it in this room where the Children's Summit met scarcely a year ago. Do you remember all the promises made on that occasion to the children of the world? Did somebody say then that Cuban children were excluded from that promise? This document contains a list of spare parts, some of them very small and inexpensive. Their only use is in children's hospitals. We're not speaking about toys but of indispensable parts to equipment for treating children with cardiac conditions. These spare parts have only one defect: they are made in the United States. I am certain that all U.S. embassies have a copy of this list and that is the reason for the increasing problems we are facing in purchasing these products around the world. Some of our colleagues have said that this item before the General Assembly is very sensitive. Is there any doubt? Among other things it puts each and every one of us to the test regarding our sensitivity to the right of all children to live... This blockade is an international problem and it's absolutely legitimate for the General Assembly to consider it. This Assembly cannot avoid its moral and political obligation to contribute to the immediate cessation of a policy that, apart from being illegal, seriously damages an entire nation.

With that, Alarcón convinced the General Assembly that international scrutiny of the blockade merited priority placement on the following year's agenda.

In an interview the following day with the Mexican news agency, Thomas Pickering, the U.S. ambassador to the United Nations, said that Cuba withdrew the resolution "because it hadn't sufficient support." He also characterized Alarcón's case against the blockade as "infested with pure lies." Alarcón countered with a press conference of his own where he accused

Pickering of "living on another planet" and stressed that Cuba had neither withdrawn the resolution or given up the fight. By postponing the discussion to 1992, Alarcón said he hoped it would give Cuba's supporters the time to press for an open debate at the General Assembly. He quoted from the official diplomatic note presented to the U.S. State Department by the Irish Embassy on behalf of the European Community, stating that:

> The Community is still of the view that the United States has no basis in international law to claim the right to license non-United States transactions with Cuba by companies incorporated outside the USA whatever their ownership or control.

When asked about support from Latin America, Alarcón asserted that Cuba had very good relations with the vast majority of countries, including the Rio Group. Their actions, he said, prove that they don't support the blockade. He referred to a recent statement by the so-called Group of Three — Columbia, Mexico and Venezuela — that pledged their help in solving "the problems Cuba experienced with some countries." Immediately after that declaration from the three Latin American presidents, Alarcón reported that the U.S. State Department reiterated its government's opposition to any move in that direction. Cuba, said Alarcón, has always been prepared to sit down with Washington over any outstanding and legitimate bilateral issue, but only on the clear understanding that such talks be held "on an equal basis, with respect for the sovereignty of both States." As the first step in that direction, Alarcón explained that Washington would need to lift its policy of blockade against Cuba.

Answering a correspondent who quoted the State Department position that the embargo is a bilateral matter and outside of United Nations' jurisdiction, Alarcón underscored the countless times the UN has made bilateral issues its business.

> However, this is not a bilateral problem. It's an attempt by the United States to interfere in the sovereign decisions of other countries. No serious government would accept that argument and that's why the United States — despite the fact that it's not one of the General Assembly's weaker members — failed to get

the General Assembly to drop the item. The item will continue to be a top priority at the United Nations for as long as the blockade exists.

Alarcón then assailed new legislative moves in the U.S. Congress such as the "Mack Amendment", which aims to prohibit the Treasury and Commerce departments from issuing licenses authorizing foreign subsidiary trade with Cuba. To begin with, he said, the United States has no right to decide whether a foreign company could trade with another country or not. But, adding insult to injury, Mack was "a very original guy" who thinks he can dictate how trade should be conducted in Britain, Canada, Switzerland and around the world.

Alarcón was also asked to explain how Cuba manages to conduct business with, for example, Spain, Britain, Japan, Venezuela, Brazil and Mexico if in fact the country is blockaded by Washington.

> Not everybody abides by the blockade, which proves that it is not 100 percent successful. The United States has not succeeded in forcing everybody to violate international law, or to accept the imposition of its will. But there is a blockade, as there is a policy to punish those who trade and those interested in having links with Cuba.

The bottom line, he said, is that:

> There exists an effort to isolate Cuba economically. To what extent it is successful is another question. It has never been completely successful.

A range of U.S. allies concur that the blockade against Cuba is bad business. For example France — hoping for an increase in the $80 million in trade with the island in 1991 — has just doubled Cuba's trade credits from $50 million to $100 million. French firms are currently involved in oil exploration, selling Cuban sugar and other agricultural products abroad, communications and training Cubans in trade and business management. When France's Budget Minister Michel Charasse visited Cuba in August 1992, he extended an extra $6 million in aid, professed that the best way for Cuba to repay its debt to France is by helping the island overcome its present difficulties, promised that Paris would assist Cuba in getting credits from the European Community, and indicated that he didn't think much of Washington's policy of "isolating or strangling Cuba."[32] Philippe Peltier, the French ambassador to Cuba, seems to indicate that Europe may be running out of patience in relation to what he calls Washington's "weak point":

> It's inappropriate to attempt to impose models of democracy on other countries... There is no reason to prefer confrontation over dialogue when differences exist... France's position is no different than Germany's or Britain's: we are quite united in rejecting any part of the Torricelli legislation — or of the blockade in general — that does not adhere to international law... There is a problem between Europe and the United States and between France and the U.S.. in terms of what we like to call the United States' weak point: its propensity to impose its legislation on other countries. That is unacceptable! One country cannot be subject to the legislation of another. There is also the principle of freedom of international trade, which we defend along with Cuba... Our businesses want to be able to trade with all countries without any outside interference. [33]

It is only the U.S. government that maintains an official "no trade" policy with Cuba. In fact, Havana has established diplomatic ties with 146 nations:

---

[32] *Granma International*, September 8, 1992.

[33] Radio Havana Cuba, August 24 and September 11, 1992.

Afghanistan
Albania
Algeria
Angola
Arab Sahara
Argentina
Armenia
Australia
Austria
Azerbaijan
Bahamas
Bangladesh
Barbados
Belarus
Belgium
Belize
Benin
Bolivia
Botswana
Brazil
Britain
Bulgaria
Burkina Faso
Burundi
Cambodia
Cameroon
Canada
Cape Verde
Chad
Chile
China
Colombia
Comoros
Congo
Cote d'Ivoire
Croatia
Cyprus
Czechia & Slovakia
Denmark
Dominica

Ecuador
Egypt
Equatorial Guinea
Estonia
Ethiopia
Finland
France
Gabon
Gambia
Georgia
Germany
Ghana
Greece
Grenada
Guinea
Guinea-Bissau
Guyana
Haiti*
Hungary
Iceland
India
Indonesia
Iran
Iraq
Italy
Jamaica
Japan
Jordan
Kazakhstan
Kuwait
Kyrgyzstan
Laos
Lebanon
Lesotho
Liberia
Libya
Luxembourg
Madagascar
Malaysia
Maldives

Mali
Malta
Mauritania
Mauritius
Mexico
Mongolia
Mozambique
Myanmar
Namibia
Nepal
Netherlands
Nicaragua
Niger
Nigeria
North Korea
Norway
Pakistan
Palestine
Panama
Papua New Guinea
Peru
Philippines
Poland
Portugal
Qatar
Rep. of Moldova
Romania
Russian Fed.
Rwanda
Saint Lucia
St. Vincent & Grenadines
San Marino
Sao Tome Principe
Saudi Arabia
Senegal
Seychelles
Sierra Leone
Slovenia
Somalia
Spain

Sri Lanka
Sudan
Suriname
Sweden
Switzerland
Syrian Arab Rep.
Tajikistan
Tanzania
Thailand
Togo
Trinidad-Tobago
Tunisia
Turkey
Turkmenistan
Uganda
Ukraine
Uruguay
Vanuatu
Vatican
Venezuela
Vietnam
Yemen
Yugoslavia
Zaire
Zambia
Zimbabwe

*with the government of
Jean Bertrand Aristede

Cuban Response to latest embargo tightening measures

"The economic blockade of Cuba that the United States has kept up for three decades is a crime against humanity. You cannot condemn a country to no food or medicine just for ideological, racial or religious reasons."

Gonzalo García Bustillos
Venezuela's Ambassador to Cuba
June 1992

Cuba certainly had little trouble beefing up its 1992 case against the blockade. In the Spring, the White House wielded another big stick in the island's direction. On a Saturday afternoon, Bush emerged from a meeting at his Maine retreat with the head of the Cuban American National Foundation[34] to announce

---

[34] CANF has a heavy hand in the legislation designed to internationalize the embargo, such as the Torricelli Bill that — as a package — will sanction third countries and penalize U.S. subsidiaries trading with Cuba. CANF has also been the subject of scrutiny by human rights groups such as Americas Watch, charging the organization with suppressing freedom of speech within the Cuban American community. Alarcón has characterized CANF as "an aggressive and very vocal minority of Cuban Americans who live in a

a new "Executive Order" against Cuba and its regional trading partners. Before informing the U.S. public, George Bush had already handed his Treasury officials instructions to close U.S. ports to all foreign vessels "carrying goods or passengers to or from Cuba" beginning April 24.[35] In addition, the new ban would be extended to third-country vessels carrying goods in which Cuba has any "interest." In a subsequent statement to the U.S. Congress, Bush revealed that the new executive order is "meant to discourage companies from increasing trade with Cuba and limit the development of tourism."

According to Cuba's legal experts the new measures — as their predecessors — disregard international law.

> They seek to discourage Cuba's export of its own products and its import of third-country products by disrupting natural shipping routes and driving up freight costs... [and] discourage third-country companies from purchasing Cuban-origin articles for use in the manufacture of their own exports... There is no pretense whatsoever that the closing of United States ports to third-country vessels, or the avowed United States "policy of economic and political isolation" of which it is a part, is in response to any activity of Cuba in the international sphere or is in any way related to the security interests of the U.S.[36]

Eleven days before the proclamation, hints of the new sanctions had reached Canada and the European Community. A joint protest note was lodged with the State Department and Ottawa issued a second reprimand after the rumor was confirmed, labeling it a "penalty" for nations trading with Cuba and advising the United States to steer clear of Canadian affairs. Letters to the editor, written by Cuba observers, appeared in a number of European papers. Like the one that follows, written by

---

Florida limbo, who think that history can be turned back so that they can live once more in Cuba in order to dominate its land and factories as well as their brothers and sisters. That was a nightmare that no one in Cuba is prepared to allow to happen again.

[35] 57 Federal register 15216. April 24, 1992.

[36] *See* page 104 for the complete text of a legal study on the executive order, as submitted to the United Nations August 26, 1992.

four leading British scientists and published in London's *Guardian* newspaper on July 22, 1992, they condemned the new sanctions as another example of by Washington's meddling in the affairs of other nations:

U.S. SANCTIONS ARE CRIPPLING CUBA

...We would also like to draw your readers' attention to a matter which we believe deserves their concern: namely the embargo imposed by the American government on all trade with its small non-threatening socialist neighbor, Cuba.

Imposed 30 years ago, the U.S. blockade has now been relentlessly tightened by a ban which forbids any vessel that has docked in Cuban ports from putting in to any American port. This, on top of other drastic trade and travel restrictions, has meant a virtual state of siege for Cuba, resulting in shortages of every kind from petrol to medicaments, machine parts to laboratory instruments. Russia no longer sends the oil formerly exchanged for sugar and, though China has helped to mitigate the petrol shortage by sending thousands of bicycles, the transport situation is now lamentable.

The lack of medicines and equipment is a very serious handicap for the once excellent Cuban health service. In May, the director of a leading medical research institute in Havana sent British friends an urgent request for various strains of influenza virus, to enable this team to carry on their important research. There is also a list of basic drugs, supplies of which are required immediately if health standards are not to drop.

The Cubans are immensely and justifiably proud of their public health record and want to carry on the great advances made since 1960; they also want to trade freely, on an equal footing with every other nation. They view the U.S. embargo as an act of war and cannot understand why it is tolerated by the international community.

We suggest that our own government should protest against the embargo to the American government, to the United Nations and to the European Community. Cuba is being treated most unfairly by having sanctions imposed — sanctions which deprive innocent people of the basic needs for a decent life, all in the name of freedom and democracy.

Patrick Collinson, F.B.A. [Regius Professor of Modern History, Univ. of Cambridge]; Stephen Hawking, O.H., O.B.E., F.R.S. [Lucasian Prof. of Math., Univ. of Cambridge]; Joseph Needham, O.H., F.R.S., F.B.A.; M.R. Pollock, F.R.S., M.D. [Emeritus Professor of Biology, University of Edinburgh].

In Havana, the Foreign Ministry issued on April 22, 1992, its own blistering condemnation of what it charges is modern-day piracy on the open seas.

On April 18, 1992 George Bush made a statement in which he reaffirmed his intention to further tighten the economic, commercial and financial embargo against Cuba.

The statement comes at a time when criticism of this hostile policy is becoming more pronounced than ever before among broad sectors of world public opinion, one of the main purposes of the statement being to hamper the efforts of those who oppose that policy.

It is odd that, at a time when opposition to the U.S. embargo against Cuba is gaining force among men, women and official and non-governmental organizations representing the most diverse currents of opinion, the president of the United States should make a statement in which he takes so opposite a position.

The facts are so obvious that even Washington officials have admitted to them in their public remarks.

A recent example is the statement made by a representative of the State Department, Mr. Robert Gelbard, at a hearing conducted in the United States Congress on April 8.

On that occasion, Gelbard told the legislators that "some Governments" agreed that Cuba should not receive any aid, but that "very few" favored the imposition of what he called an embargo on the island.

The growing attention paid by world public opinion to this matter was also highlighted towards the end of 1991, when the United Nations General Assembly decided at its 46th session to include in its agenda an item entitled "Necessity of ending the economic, commercial and financial embargo imposed by the United States of America against Cuba."

As everyone knows, this item will be open for discussion at

the meetings of the General Assembly's session this year.

One of the arguments advanced by the United States delegation to the United Nations in its attempt to prevent inclusion of the item on the agenda was that the issue was one of a bilateral embargo — consistent with the provisions of international law — and not a blockade.

Even though there are numerous United States provisions currently in force and from years past which demonstrate conclusively how the White House has been trying to extend its jurisdiction beyond its own territory in order to impose its laws, orders and regulations on Cuba, Bush's most recent pronouncement on the subject is of singular significance in this context.

The president makes no attempt to conceal his intention of imposing on Cuba a political, economic and social order which is consistent with Washington's interests, while, without shrinking from hinting at reprisals against countries which do not toe this line, he casts himself in the role of leader of a crusade in which "my administration will continue to stress to the Governments of the entire world" the necessity of isolating the island economically.

In this context and without the slightest moral — or diplomatic, for that matter — hesitation, Bush proclaimed his intention of violating the recognized principle of freedom of the seas when he stated that he had instructed the Department of the Treasury to issue regulations prohibiting vessels engaging in trade with Cuba from entering United States ports.

The United States chief executive has openly violated the internationally recognized rules of law in accordance with which no State may employ pressure, coercion or any other actions in restraint of free merchant shipping and freedom of navigation.

This aggressive stance, together with other foreign policy actions in the early years of the 1990s, further indicates how the United States Government understands the so-called new world order, while at the same time it sounds a warning that Washington may be seeking to mount a naval blockade against Cuba which would have incalculable consequences.

And this is happening precisely at a time when in many places around the world in a massive, fraternal joining together of people of all races and beliefs, people are pledging their willingness to stand by Cuba's side to send — as the promoters have said — an oil tanker or a ship carrying medicines or powdered milk to our people who are stoically bearing the brunt of a double embargo, especially the embargo which Bush is seeking to tighten further in the name of opening a channel between us and the so-called "peaceful transition to democracy."

The United States president knows that the ships which he is trying to prevent from reaching Cuba have on board foodstuffs and medicines for the Cuban people, and supplies needed to light our homes, to harvest our sugar crop or to keep our school system operating.

Cuba's ministry of foreign affairs believes that the statement by the president of the United States which contains the ideas described above has undoubtedly performed the service of highlighting the brutal reality of the economic, trade and financial embargo against our country, and at the same time it has shown the President to be a public instigator of illegal actions violating time-honored legal norms observed by civilized Governments and nations.

In addition to the open seas, the U.S. blockade has for years deemed the skies out of Cuba's reach. The U.S. Federal Civil Aeronautics Administration forbids Cuban passenger planes from flying over U.S. airspace, edging Cubana Airline commercial flights to Canada and the Caribbean out of normal air corridors. The ban not only violates the international convention on civil aviation but also annually costs Cuba more than $1.5 million in extra fuel. If Cuba were to respond in kind, U.S. airline companies would be forced to spend some $30 million in rerouting the more than 35,000 flights over the island's airspace. In 1989, the U.S Treasury Department also refused to allow Cubana permission to fly commercial charter flights between Havana and Miami, citing the trade embargo as the reason. U.S.-owned charters make the trip every day.

"Intimidation, threats and pressure"

"There can be no new world order without justice and equality... nations must learn to listen to and respect one another. A new world order must be achieved through the search for consensus among nations."

Carlos Salinas de Gurtari
Mexican President

"We regret to inform you..." — a phrase Cubans complain that they hear far too often. It is an apology from a foreign supplier who went to fill a Cuban sales order only to be told by the U.S. Treasury Department's Office of Export License that the island is off-limits. Sometimes accompanying the "Dear Juan" letter is the paperwork of a contract cancelled by a foreign firm that followed U.S. set procedure and applied for a license to export a U.S.-made replacement part for equipment already in operation on the island. Ricardo Alarcón, the Cuban Foreign Minister, could not remember the last time Treasury approved what would be a routine request if not for Washington's trade ban with his country. Other times, Treasury officials scramble to stay one step ahead of Cuban trade interests as in the case of the memo Washington recently distributed to every member of the Swiss Chamber of Commerce:

> The United States government understands that the Government of Cuba may be offering foreign investors the opportunity to purchase land, manufacturing facilities, tourist

resorts and other assets in Cuba that belong to, or are the subject of outstanding claims by American or other foreign nationals. The Cubans may also be offering joint venture partnerships.

The United States originally imposed an economic embargo in 1962, after Cuba nationalized some 1.8 billion 1962 dollars worth of U.S.-owned property without paying prompt, adequate, and effective compensation, as required under international law. That embargo remains in effect.

There are 5,911 separate American claims pending against the Government of Cuba. These claims are today valued at over $5 billion, including 6 percent interest [per] annum.

U.S. claims against Cuba remain unsettled. We expect many of the claims will be actively pursued when U.S.-Cuban relations are normalized. As a result of Cuba's support for insurgency abroad, policies of internal repression, and lack of democratic institutions, the United States does not have full diplomatic or commercial relations with Cuba.

The United States government strongly urges business firms to avoid entering into contracts with the Government of Cuba, or investing in the Cuban economy, where such actions would involve assets located in Cuba that may be legally encumbered by unresolved claims to such assets by American citizens...

To this end, business firms are encouraged to contact: The Foreign Claims Settlement Commission of the United States, 601 D Street, N.W., Washington, DC, 20579...

Cuba takes exception to Washington's spin on the history of the broken bilateral relations. Alarcón asserts that:

[The Cuban government] always stood ready to make good on that promise [of settling the American claims]... In fact we have compensated everyone except the U.S. corporations. And that was not our fault... The U.S. government didn't accept our formulas for compensation which matched our reality at that time... It's true that we nationalized their holdings on the island, but U.S. law prohibited them from taking compensation from Havana. You would think the United States Government would have tried to protect the interest of those companies in much the same way a number of Western European countries did. Those European powers didn't blockade Cuba, didn't invade Cuba, didn't try to topple our government. They simply negotiated and settled with us — Spain, Switzerland, Britain, France. Everyone except the United States. It's even ironic now to see how, over the years, we've developed economic links with some of the companies that were nationalized back in the early 1960s. [37]

Alarcón does however agree with the United States government that any future negotiations would need to step back in time, beginning with Cuba's nationalization laws. Yet, Cuba has its own financial scores to settle that start at a $40 billion pricetag for the blockade — not including the cost of Washington's other anti-Cuba policies.

In any negotiations, Cuba would need to discuss our counter claims. The U.S.-inspired Bay of Pigs invasion cost us dearly. The economic blockade has cost us billions of dollars. In the best legal tradition of the West, Cuba has a legitimate claim for compensation for the damage caused by the economic embargo. This just can't be forgotten. It's naive to assume that only the United States has points to negotiate. If we were to now sit down and begin talks, the scale would be tipped in our favor. The United States has much more to compensate than Cuba. But while the United States would have to pay the Cuban people damages, some U.S. companies would also benefit from the negotiations. So it would be a rather complex negotiating process in which we would be prepared to compensate those companies — as I have told them many times — but we would also need to be compensated for the damages caused not by the companies but the government that represents them. One day, I hope to see Cuba and the United States sitting down to iron out these problems. [38]

Until that time, the Cold War rages on... In the Spring of 1992,

---

[37] *See* Franklin's *The Cuban Revolution and the United States* for the detailed history.

[38] *Cuba and the United States,* May 1992.

when U.S. Agriculture Secretary Ed Madigan learned that India planned to sell rice to Cuba, he rushed to President Bush to advise that New Delhi be scratched off the list of countries authorized to make wheat purchases from the United States — setting off a storm of protest in India and within the U.S. farmbelt. One Midwest grain firm executive likened Madigan to a clown: "I think USDA's statements on this matter are bozo-type statements." Another farming executive blasted Madigan for his bad trade policy: "A USDA secretary should not argue against any reasonable trade initiative that will boost U.S. farm exports. The USDA needs to just shut up." Madigan essentially took that advise in the face of India's decision to go ahead and sell Cuba 10,000 tons of rice on a deferred payment credit of 360 days.

Others are also willing to weather Washington's fury to take advantage of the new opportunities Cuba is offering traders. David Jessop of the Anglo-Cuban Trade Council in London told IPS news service that he expects to see a substantial growth in Britain-Cuba trade. He advises British companies to move fast because of the "enormous" and "tantalizing" opportunities emerging on the island. Jessop refused to disclose the names of British financiers flirting with the island following "concern about reports that the U.S. authorities may attempt to pressure British firms to prevent them from doing business with Cuba." The strict secrecy emerged after the companies that travelled to Cuba during 1992 complained that they had been harassed by U.S. authorities who "had hinted that any decision to invest in Cuba could affect their operation in the United States." While currently there is no direct British investment in Cuba, Britain exported to Cuba $56 million in goods in 1991. That figure jumped during the first half of 1992, up 34 percent ($34.3 million) over the same period in 1991.[39] Companies from Canada, Ecuador, Nicaragua, Mexico, Venezuela, Spain and other European countries reached their own investment agreements with Cuba's heavy industry sector during 1991-92, signing a wide range of

---

[39] Various reports from Inter Press Service and Radio Havana Cuba, September 11, 1992. Britain, however, is in a unique position given that Cuba has lost some 70 percent of its purchasing power over the last two years and 1992 imports are expected to drop 58 percent when compared with 1989 purchases.

contracts including with the island's state petroleum company, Cupet, and in the nickel industry, again working at full capacity after a temporary lull in 1991 caused by the abrupt shortfall in Soviet oil deliveries. Trade officials report that foreign companies are also in the market to invest in copper, lead, zinc, chemicals, fertilizers and developing Cuba's alternative energy industry. Foreign investments in tourism are providing relatively quick returns, with Spanish companies recovering their initial investment in less than five years. That has caught the eye of other business groups — such as Mexico's DSC with a $14 million interest in the five-star Tuxpan Hotel located on the sands of Varadero Beach.[40] The 1992 trade protocol between Cuba and China calls for island deliveries of nickel in exchange for Chinese exports of food, medicines, bicycles and machinery spare parts.

For decades the Nonaligned Nations Movement (NAM) — as a voice of Third World diplomacy — has addressed different aspects of the U.S.-Cuba conflict. At its 10th Summit held in Jakarta, Indonesia in September 1992, the final declaration urges Washington to end its "hostile actions" against Cuba, lift the 30-year blockade and vacate Guantánamo Bay — now occupied by the U.S. Navy. In what is the most comprehensive resolution NAM has ever passed regarding U.S. actions against Cuba, its 108 member countries also condemned Pentagon violations of Cuban waters and airspace, and the broadcast of agitational and illegal radio and television programs to the Caribbean nation. This condemnation flowed from the spirit of the Jakarta Message — a call to democratize international relations. It recognized that with the "collapse of the bipolar structure of the world... interdependence, integration and globalization of the world economy" are realities in today's world along with "interference in the internal affairs of States [and] policies of hegemony and domination." NAM reaffirmed its beliefs that "no country... should use its power to dictate its concept of democracy and human rights or to impose conditionalities on others," while

---

[40] Press conference by Abraham Maciques, general manager of Cubanacan, the island's tourism development group, May 6, 1992, where he reported that the Tuxpan Hotel earned over $6 million during the first quarter of 1992.

offering "dialogue and negotiation" as the mechanism to peacefully resolve any and all bilateral and regional disputes.

Addressing the 40 heads of states and 108 government delegations, United Nations Secretary-General Boutros Boutros-Ghali warned that the end of the Cold War has not brought a halt to what he described as the "phenomenon of power... the temptation of some states to dominate either globally or regionally." Agreeing, the head of the Cuban delegation pointed to U.S. policy against his country. Cuban Vice-President Juan Almeida observed:

> We are the only country in the world subjected to the merciless iron grip of an economic, trade, technical and cultural blockade for over 30 years... Today, when the Cold War and confrontation is said to no longer exist, the United States is attempting to force third nations to actively participate in this inhumane policy... tremendous pressure is being exerted throughout the world to keep our country from obtaining fuel, receiving credit, or simply trading.[41]

Almeida charged that Washington has with a vengeance stepped up the blockade in order to exacerbate Cuban shortages.

> By making the blockade even tighter and more oppressive than ever, the United States hopes to create such severe conditions of misery and hunger that our people will finally surrender... We could ask ourselves on what ethical and moral bases can [the blockade] be carried out? What laws back them up?... How can they talk about human rights when they are trying to starve a whole people?[42]

Picking up those threads a few days later, Cuban President Fidel Castro asked his nation:

> Where did [the collapse of the socialist camp] hit us hardest? On the economic front... Changes in prices... what we once

---

[41] September 1, 1992, addressing the inaugural session on behalf of the Latin American and Caribbean region.
[42] Ibid.

received from the socialist countries for our exports compared to current world market prices... for sugar... we have lost $2.469 billion [from the Soviet Union] and $270.5 million from Eastern Europe; in nickel, we have lost $30 million; in other products, $14.4 million. In terms of annual credit losses, taking into account that we never receive credits from the World Bank or the U.S.-controlled international financial institutions, [we have lost] $1.463 billion; and in terms of credit lines with Eastern Europe, $162 million... from the Soviet International Investment Bank, $13 million. In terms of increased prices on our exports, we are losing another $80 million. Difficulties in finding alternative markets, in citrus for example, have cost us $144.6 million; in other products, $55 million. In total we are losing $4.701 billion — and these are only the direct trade losses. Indirect losses... account for another $1 billion. All this adds up to approximately $5.7 billion annually between 1989 and 1992. This means that... we have lost 70 percent of our purchasing power.[43]

On the blockade, he assailed Washington for:

...further intensifying its blockade, working on new measures against Cuba that would even harm the sovereignty of third countries. They aren't satisfied and want to throw up even bigger obstacles for our country: they do everything possible to keep us from buying fuel on the international market, and try even harder to keep us from having the money to pay for the little fuel we are receiving; they hound every small attempt that Cuba makes to increase its exports; they hound every effort that Cuba makes to export new products we are developing; they are attacking our economy as never before... This is why now, under these conditions, the U.S. blockade does more harm than ever before. In 1960, when the United States took its first measures against Cuba, one ton of sugar bought some 8 tons of oil; now, one ton of sugar at the so-called world market prices only buys 1.4 tons of oil... [44]

---

[43] September 5, 1992, speaking in Cienfuegos, Cuba.
[44] Ibid.

In an earlier speech to the Ibero-American Summit in Madrid, the Cuban leader charged the United States with a "policy of genocide." He went on to say that "the United States is trying to economically smother Cubans, use hunger to bring us to our knees."[45] As in his address to the 1st Ibero-American Summit one year earlier, Fidel Castro underscored Latin American unity as the way out not for Cuba alone but for the region's underdevelopment. Along those same lines, the majority of the heads of state who addressed the Nonaligned Summit in Jakarta stressed south-south cooperation as an essential building block of Third World growth.

Exploring south-south trade with Cuba, representatives from 18 developing nations attended a four-day meeting in Havana in the Spring of 1992. They passed their own resolution denouncing any type of blockade or economic coercion to infringe on the free flow of trade. Raúl Portocarrero, manager of the Peruvian firm EXIMAC S.R., urged "Latin America to stick together" and form joint ventures as he related how the transnationals spearheaded a campaign in his country to discredit Cuban-made medicines which sell at lower prices than U.S. pharmaceuticals.[46]

The United States has also been displeased by regional efforts to bring Cuba closer to its Caribbean neighbors. In June 1992, Cuba attended the 13th Caribbean Community Summit as an official observer when one of CARICOM's standing committees recommended expanding membership to include Cuba plus other nations bordering the Caribbean Sea. As Cuba made a bid for membership into the Caribbean Trade Organization (CTO), the United States tried to block its entry with the scare tactic that,

> ...Cuba has been seeking tourism investments from many of the same sources current CTO Members tap, but Cuba may not currently be under the same business and labor regulatory constraints as its neighbors. Cuba, therefore, may offer tourism

---

[45] July 23, 1992, Madrid, Spain.

[46] Radio Havana Cuba, May 14, 1992. The meeting was sponsored by the UN Conference on Trade and Development (UNCTAD), which stressed that Third World products are often relegated to a back seat by competing U.S. companies with the resources the Third World doesn't have to aggressively market their wares.

investors a better return, at least initially, than other countries
in the area. We urge you to keep Cuba out of the CTO until it is
a democratic nation. [47]

Putting that "advise" aside, the CTO admitted Cuba as a full-
fledged member and already the regional group has begun to
include Cuba as a stop on its Caribbean multi-destination holiday
cruises. Cuba has also renewed diplomatic ties with a number of
Caribbean states, including most recently with St. Vincent and
the Grenadines.

---

[47] Letter sent by the U.S. State Department to every Caribbean State.
Procured from a protected source.

"Twelve aspects regarding the extraterritorial nature of the embargo"

As arguments unfolded at the United Nations in 1991, the U.S. State Department stood behind its initial statement of August 21 that, "A blockade implies that the United States is taking action to prevent other countries from trading with Cuba. That is clearly not the case." Cuba countered by summarizing 12 areas in which the United States seeks extraterritorial application of the embargo policy:

1. The United States prohibits a corporation or other business entity organized under the laws of a third country and located and doing business in that country from exporting to Cuba products manufactured wholly in that third country, but which incorporate any United States component part or material. It doesn't matter if the component part or material has been completely transformed in the new product. Exceptions are possible only upon application by the third-country company, demonstrating that the U.S.-origin component parts or materials constitute 20 percent or less of the value of the product.[48]

2. The United States prohibits nationals of third countries from re-exporting United States origin goods to Cuba unless their re-exportation is specifically approved by the U.S. Department of Commerce. It is the policy and practice of the U.S. Commerce Department to deny approval. It makes no difference whether or not the third-country national originally obtained the goods for

---

[48] Taken from Federal Regulations Code 15, section 774.1 and 785.1

resale or how long the third-country national has owned the goods.[49]

3. The above restrictions apply equally to U.S. technical data — information in any form, tangible or intangible — which can be used in the design, production or manufacture of products. A third-country national may not re-export to Cuba technical data that was exported (bought and paid for) from the United States. In many instances, third-country nationals may not export products manufactured wholly in the third country and containing no U.S. components or materials simply because the original products were made using U.S. technical data.[50]

4. The United States claims the embargo may be extended to business entities located in third countries, doing business in third countries and organized under the laws of third countries if the entity is owned or controlled by U.S. corporations or persons. "Control" has been defined even when the U.S. interest constitutes less than 50 percent. Current U.S. law allows such subsidiaries to engage in import and export transactions with Cuba. However, a wide range of commercial activity is forbidden including investments in Cuba and engaging in joint ventures with the island. Regarding import-export transactions, the subsidiary must apply for a U.S. Treasury Department license before signing any contract with Cuba and must demonstrate that it operates independent of the parent company; that no one from the head office will be involved in the transaction; that the transaction does not involve money from a U.S. account or U.S. financing; and that any financing or credit extension by the subsidiary will comply with U.S. Treasury Department regulations.[51]

5. The embargo applies to any third-country company with Cuban nationals on the payroll. They are prohibited from having any financial or commercial dealings with the United States or U.S. nationals. Any property the company may have in the United States will be frozen.[52]

---

[49] Taken from Federal Regulations Code 15, section 774.1

[50] Taken from Federal Regulations Code 15, sections 779.1; 779.8; 779.4.

[51] Taken from Federal Regulations Code 31, sections 515.559; 515.329; testimony by the Director of the Office of Foreign Assets Control before the U.S. Congress on August 2, 1989.

[52] Federal Regulations Code 31, section 515.302.

6. Third country banks are banned from maintaining dollar accounts for Cuba or Cuban nationals; the embargo also prohibits the third-country firm from using U.S. currency or money from a dollar account.[53]

7. The embargo prohibits the importation of third-country goods if a part of any component originated in Cuba, including raw material that has been totally transformed in the manufacturing process.[54]

8. The above prohibition applies to products including a component that originated in Cuba even when Cuba no longer supplies the material and regardless of how long the material has been owned by the third-country company or national.[55]

9. By executive order, the United States maintains a "blacklist" of hundreds of third-country corporations and firms that U.S. nationals and companies are barred from engaging with in any financial transactions. These companies are deemed "specially designated" nationals of Cuba, acting on behalf of the government of Cuba or is owned or controlled by the government of Cuba.[56] On occasion, the United States has taken a name off the blacklist after effective protest by the targeted company or its government. However, such companies will think twice before again engaging in trade with Cuba.

10. By U.S. law, Washington's representatives on all international financial institutions are required to oppose granting loans or other financial support to Cuba. These bodies include the Inter-American Bank, the International Bank for Reconstruction and Development, the International Development Association and the International Monetary Fund.[57]

11. The U.S. Congress recently approved the Mack Amendment, measures that call for extending the embargo to all

---

[53] U.S. State Department briefing to Latin American embassies on July 12, 1963; Deputy Secretary of the Treasury Robert Carswell addressing the Conference on the Internationalization of the Capital Markets, March 1981; Comptroller General's Report to the U.S. Congress, November 14, 1980.

[54] Federal Regulations Code 31, section 515.204.

[55] Ibid.

[56] Federal Regulations Code 31, section 515.306.

[57] United States Code 22, sections 283r; 284; 286aa.

U.S. subsidiaries; President Bush, by executive order, has prohibited foreign vessels that stop in Cuban ports from entering the United States; other Congressional moves would deny U.S. aid to any country which furnishes assistance to Cuba; and still others target by name Cuba's current trade partners.

12. The policy of the United States is to pressure third-country governments and companies to sever trade ties with Cuba or face the consequences. [58]

---

[58] This has been well-documented by researchers and journalists in the United States, Cuba and other countries. Alarcón refers to, as one source, "Cuba Woos Capitalists Feebly, Driven by Need Instead of Desire." *Wall Street Journal,* September 11, 1991, pp. A-13.

Examples of blockaded trade deals

Embargo or blockade? For the still undecided, Cuba released the following list that charts the trail of broken transactions with companies from around the world, stopped in their tracks by Washington's no-trade policy with Cuba.

ARGENTINIAN FIRMS

Medix

U.S. Treasury Department refused to issue license to allow the company to sell Cuba spare parts for the machine that cleans dialysis machines and spare parts for System 4 ultrascan used in the treatment of ophthalmological conditions.

BRAZILIAN FIRMS

Vickers Inc.
November 1989
Told Cuba that they could not quote prices for hydraulic-pneumatic components because they were prohibited from selling to Cuba.

Gates Export Corporation of Brazil
January 1990
After completed negotiations on "V" transmission belts, the company told Cuba they were in no position to make a price bidding because they are considered a U.S. enterprise and outlawed from trading with the island.

Woodword
October 1990
After the Cuban enterprise Marpesca requested a price quote on

shipbuilding materials, Woodword replied that they were prohibited from supplying a bid as the company was a U.S. subsidiary and banned from selling to Cuba.

Hoechst
June 1990
Refused to sell Cuba plastic resins on the grounds that 80 percent of the manufactured product originated in the United States and that the company's request to sell to Cuba had been turned down by the Treasury Department.

Embraer
May 1991
Treasury Department prohibits the sale of five cargo planes to Cuba, arguing that the planes contained U.S.-made components. The newspaper *Folha de Sao Paulo* reports that the U.S. Treasury Department decision helped push the company into financial debt.

Dorr-Oliver Vrasil
May 1992
When Cuba went to restock filters, company officials said they were prohibited as a U.S. subsidiary from dealing with the island.

CANADIAN FIRMS

Ayerst Laboratories
June 1985
U.S. Treasury blocked products destined for Medicuba, including colyrum, which prevents gas and chemical damage to the eyes.

Cooper Tool
August-September 1984
Cancelled signed contracts #19-8065-11 and #19-0322-11 for delivery of tools.

General Electric of Canada
July 1986
Refused to sell Cuba the book "Subway electrification" because the subsidiary felt it was prohibited from having trade contact with Cuba.

Federal Pacific Electric of Canada
August 1986
Refused to export fuses because they were of U.S. origin.

Vulcan-Hart Canada Inc.
August 1986
After contract #64582 was drawn up, company said it could not supply equipment for commercial ranges because of U.S. origin.

Andrew Antenna
September 1986
The company decided after signing contract #69006-103 for the sale of electronic equipment that it would be impossible to obtain a U.S. Treasury Department license to export the products.

Do-All Canada Inc.
October 1988
Declined purchase order for metal-cutting tools that originated in the United States.

Federal Pacific Electric of Canada
May 1990
After signing contract #97736, refused to make delivery on fuses on the grounds that they were of U.S. origin.

Simonds Industries
June 1990
Refused to fill order for U.S.-acquired wood cutting tools.

Pepsi Cola Canada Ltd.
May 1991
After accepting an order from Regor International for 29,000 cases of soft drink, company refuses to fill it upon learning that the product is destined to Cuba. The company continues its refusal even after being the subject of a reprimand issued by the Canadian Trade Ministry. That censure, written on June 7, 1991, and signed by R. H. Davidson, director general of the Ministry's Latin American and Caribbean Bureau, stated: "As we understand the situation... at a meeting on May 17, 1991, Mr. Saint Germain of Regor was told by Mr. Sbrollini, regional manager of Pepsi

Cola Montreal, that the order would not be filled where Cuba was the ultimate destination and that this decision resulted from discussions between senior officials of Pepsi Cola Montreal and the U.S. head office of Pepsi Cola. It was later suggested by Mr. Sbrollini that the price quotation was wrong and that a considerably higher (and uneconomical) price would be required for the order to be processed... Canadian government policy, which we would expect to be supported by companies incorporated in Canada, favors trade in non-strategic goods with Cuba. The Canadian government has also consistently opposed the extraterritorial application of U.S. trade policy towards Cuba, either directly by the U.S. government or through U.S. parent corporations. As such, the possible interference by the U.S. head office of Pepsi Cola in this matter, resulting in the cancellation of a Canadian export order, would be a matter of considerable concern."

Hercules Canada Inc.
May 1991
After trading with Cuba, the firm communicated that they could no longer continue doing business with the island because 80 percent of the basic component of the cellophane Cuba was interested in buying was now coming from the United States. The firm also noted that they had requested permission to continue sales to Cuba but had been turned down.

Hobart Canada Inc.
May-June 1991
Cancelled an order through the Canadian Commercial Corporation for airplane kitchen equipment.

Servispec Prolux
June 1991
After successful negotiations with Cuban enterprise Consumimport for the sales of industrial light bulbs, Servispec noted on contract "U.S.-origin merchandise is prohibited."

Conval Quebec
August 1991
Responded to the Cuban enterprise, Cubaequipos, that they were

in no position to bid on an order for electrical supplies and regulators because the products of the Canadian firm originate with the U.S. company American Switch Co, Ltd.

Nedco
August 1991
Refused to supply material for electrical installations on the grounds that the products are of U.S. origin.

Furnes Electric
August 1991
Refused to quote a price for electrical accessories as products are of U.S. origin.

Square D
August 1991
After doing business with Cuba for years, the company surprised Cuban officials by announcing that they could not ship electrical switches to the island because the firm is a U.S. subsidiary.

Diamond Canapower
September 1991
Refused to quote a price for boiler components because all products of U.S. origin.

Lennox Industries
October 1991
Told Cuba that as a company owned 100 percent by the U.S. parent, Lennox, the Canadian subsidiary was instructed to obey the trade embargo against Cuba and could not sell the island industrial refrigeration equipment.

Dow Chemical Vickford Industries
1991
Told Cuban buyers that they needed to request price quotings on material needed in the production of phone cables directly from main office in the United States.

Loctite Canada Inc.
Cancelled three signed contracts to supply glue for motor

couplings, after learning that the destination was Cuba.

FRENCH FIRMS

CGR Thompson Group
The U.S. Treasury Department refused to issue license to this U.S. subsidiary of General Electric to sell Cuba spare parts for x-ray equipment widely used throughout the island.

GERMAN FIRMS

Siemens AG
U.S. Treasury Department refuses licenses to company to sell Cuba Gamma Cameras, a piece of equipment used in nuclear medicine to determine pathologies and, as such, saves the patient surgery; Ultrasound with Color Doppler, SI-1200 Sonoline used to diagnose cardiovascular diseases; Magnetic Nuclear Resonance System used to determine pathologies that cannot be found through other means.

ITALIAN FIRMS

Dow Chemical Co. Ltd.
1991
The Italian group which had regular trade with Cuba sold the production line of resins used in water treatment to Dow. Because of this, they said they were now under Dow instructions and that the parent company had issued orders not to sell to Cuba.

JAPANESE FIRMS

Toshiba Corporation
U.S. Treasury Department refused to issue license to allow the sale of SSH-65A Ultrasound with Color Doppler, a piece of diagnostic equipment for cardiovascular diseases. The company was also prohibited from selling Neuropack IV Potential Recalling Equipment used to study neuro-physiological pathologies.

MEXICAN FIRMS

Crouse-Hinds Domex
October 1984
Refused to give price quote for iron connections used in electric

installations because the product is not manufactured locally. The company is a U.S. subsidiary.

Industria Fotográfica Interamericana, S.A.
May 1991
As a subsidiary of Eastman Kodak the company stated that it could not sell Cuba photographic supplies because it was bound to adhering to the U.S. embargo of Cuba.

Coca Cola, Mexico
Claiming that the company was bound to follow the letter of the embargo law, the subsidiary refused to sell Cuba 28,000 sodas for the Organizing Committee of the VI World Athletic Cup, meeting in Cuba in September 1992.

Mexican Sugar Imports
April 1992
The U.S. Treasury Department sought guarantees that Mexico would not sell Cuban sugar to the United States as part of a commercial accord between the two countries.

SPANISH FIRMS
Piher Semiconductors, S.A.
U.S. Treasury Department placed the company on a blacklist and sued it selling Cuba U.S.-made equipment for a semiconductor plant being built in Pinar del Rio. After agreeing to a settlement of $1 million in 1985, the company filed for bankruptcy two years later.

SWEDISH FIRMS
Alfa-Laval
May 1991
Medicuba placed an order for replacement cartridges for a Swedish-manufactured filtration system the company had previously sold to Cuba. The system contained filtration cartridges manufactured in the United States. The company was forced to cancel contract #15-6-2-06772-418-R-5983 after the U.S. Treasury Department denied its application under U.S. Exports Administration Regulations, section 773.7.(b).(1), which prohibits the export or re-export of spare parts to Cuba. In a letter

to Medicuba, Alfa-Laval representative Tina Kristensen writes: "We have now applied for a license from the United States government concerning possible export of U.S. originated membranes to you. We did what we could, but there seems to be nothing we can do in order to obtain the license. Enclosed please find material sent to us from Romicon, U.S., who led the investigation for us. Material [copies of the above law] which clearly states why we cannot export the goods to you. We therefore regret to inform you that we are obliged to turn down your order for replacement cartridges for Medicuba."

Siemens Elena AB
U.S. Treasury Department refused to issue a license to allow the company to sell Cuba a Sicard 400 Intelligent Electrocardiograph, used in detecting heart diseases.

LKB Pharmaceuticals
U.S. Treasury Department refused to issue license to allow the company to sell Cuba laboratory equipment used to determine hormone and protein levels in the blood.

Visa denials:
bricks in the wall

"Regardless of political ideologies, Cuba surgical techniques that benefit patients and can improve their lives should be shared by all people and all countries. Especially noted is Dr. Rodrigo Alvarez Cambras' work with children to correct deformity as well as lengthen bones, so that the legs will be the same length and patients can walk more normally. This transcends political problems between countries, which I believe personally are not going to last much longer."

Dr. Anthony Serustini
orthopedic surgeon
University of Nevada
June 1992

Once upon a time, the visitor had a choice of travel between Cuba and the United States: the daring boarded the air shuttle while the economy rider grabbed a seat on the ferry. Today, U.S. travel restrictions to Cuba amount to one thing: "No trespassing." Technically, it's not illegal to travel to Cuba from the United States. What U.S. citizens cannot do is engage in "Trading with the Enemy." That means — for even the most adventurous who might try surfing or parachuting to the island — you will still be breaking the law once you buy a cup of coffee or pay a Cuban bus driver the 10 cents for a ride around Havana.

One U.S. fisherman is a case in point. A Texas judged ruled that Dan Snow violated the Trading with the Enemy Act by arranging for his fellow sportsmen to experience the fight of a large mouth bass, ancestors of those first brought to Cuba back in

1928 from the southern lakes of the United States. Ignoring his appeal that the embargo tramples on his constitutional right to travel, Mr. Snow is sentenced in January 1990 to serve 90 days in jail, 5 years probation, perform 1,000 hours of community service and pay a $5,000 fine. At the same time as thousands of Canadian tourists make Cuba their winter get-away, the Treasury Department regulations prohibit the average person from the United States from taking a look at the island for themselves.

Exempt from the travel restrictions are people with family in Cuba, journalists, writers and professionals conducting full-time research in their fields with a proven interest in travelling to Cuba. These chosen few are free to spend a limited amount of money in Cuba without securing on-the-spot permission from the U.S. Treasury Department, although they can be subject to questioning by U.S. customs officials on their return.

The embargo also serves to keep Cubans out of the United States, locking the door on most opportunities for professional exchanges and keeping families separated. A Havana study found that many Cuban requests to visit close relatives in the United States take up to a year or more before an answer is given. As well, of the 62,117 exit visas Cuba issued to people wanting to migrate to the United States in 1990, Washington acted on only 6 percent.

Cuban chess master Guillermo García had his own unfortunate run-in with the U.S. embargo in 1988. After winning second place at the New York Open, the U.S. Treasury Department confiscated García's $10,000 prize money, dumped it into a blocked account and told the champ that a line to the cash would only open if he left Cuba.

Below is a sampling of respected Cuban professionals invited by North American institutions or organizations to visit the United States who have been denied the right of entry:

December 1982 Florentino Cruz and Arnaldo Silva denied visas to attend a conference organized by the American Philosophical Association in Baltimore, Maryland. APA Representative, Professor Cliff Durand assails visas denial as "censorship" on the part of the U.S. State Department.
1983 Olga Finlay and Leonor Rodríguez denied visas to visit New York City under an invitation issued by City officials.

March 1986 Film director Pastor Vega denied visa to attend the Third World Film Festival in Atlanta, Georgia.

May 1986 Choreographer Rogelio Martínez is denied visa. He was to have worked with the Schomberg Center for Research in Black Culture on a project funded by a Ford Foundation Grant.

May 1986 Ten Cuban physicists denied visas to attend an international conference sponsored by the American Physical Society.

November 1986 Five orthopedic specialists denied visas to attend the Latin American Orthopedic and Traumatological Society conference in Puerto Rico.

February 1987 Artists Rebeca Chávez and Senal Paz denied visas to travel to New York City where they were to have worked with the New York-based Center for Cuban Studies on a project funded by the Ford Foundation.

January 1988 Two artists Professor Consuelo Castaneda and Arturo Cuenca denied visas on the grounds that they work for a "terrorist state."

February 1988 Tropicana dance company denied visas to tour the United States. [Because of public pressure, in April 1988 the State Department is forced to reverse this ban.]

May 1988 Cuban penal experts denied visas to visit five U.S. prisons as part of an exchange with the Washington-based Institute for Policy Studies.

October 1988 A delegation from Cuba's National Film Institute denied visas to attend the Denver (Colorado) International Film Festival.

October 1988 Another film delegation denied visas to participate at the Festival Cine San Juan in Puerto Rico.

March 1988 Havana Mayor denied visa to attend a conference on drugs in New York City sponsored by mayor's from the United States and Latin America.

April 1989 Then deputy Foreign Minister Ricardo Alarcón denied visa to attend a conference at Johns Hopkins School of Advanced International Studies.

May 1989 Theatrical director Humberto Llamas denied visa for cultural exchange.

May 1989 Orchestra Aragón denied visa to perform at a Chicago Latin music festival.

May 1989 Two athletes denied visas to compete in Puerto Rico.

August 1989 Jazz pianist Gonzalo Rubalcaba and his band Proyecto denied visas to perform in New York City.

July-August 1990 Education minister denied visa to lead a delegation of 150 Cuban athletes to the Goodwill Games in Seattle, Washington.

December 1990 Four artists denied visas to perform at a Miami concert.

February 1991 The U.S. Treasury Department refused to allow the plane Orbis, the humanitarian medical project, to fly to Cuba for a professional exchange. Orbis volunteers, including its team of ophthalmologists, had worked in over 60 countries and had planned to perform cornea transplants, glaucoma operations, refractive surgery and other operations during their 12-day stay. Four months later, Treasury lifts the travel ban on Orbis.

April 1991 A team of Cuban nuclear engineers denied visas to attend a meeting sponsored by the World Association of Nuclear Operators. The *Washington Post* blasts the State Department for denying the visas as the Cuban experts — the only guests not to attend the conference on nuclear power security measures — are working on constructing the nuclear facility in the Cuban town of Cienfuegos.

June 1991 A leading Cuban scientist, Dr. Julio Baisre, denied visa to participate in an international scientific conference in Puerto Rico.

July 1991 Cuban feminists Leonora Rodríguez, Margy Delgado and María Rodríguez denied visa to speak at a conference of the Women's International League for Peace and Freedom.

1991 Officials from Cuba's Sugar Ministry, Jesús Hernández, Manuel Paláez and Raúl Trujillo denied visas for a professional interchange with a private institution.

Educator Esther Valdés denied visa for professional visit.

Health officials Alexis Cedeño, Rubén Darío González and Carlos Alberto Guasch denied visas to attend a course on hospital administration taught in Arkansas.

Health professional Rosa Isla García denied visa to participate in a scientific health congress.

Sugar officials Roberto Armas and Rodolfo Maribona denied visas to attend as delegates a meeting of the regional Sugar Association.

Biochemist Rosa Isla denied visa to attend a scientific

gathering in Philadelphia.

Cubana Airline executives Caridad del Cristo and María Font denied visas to attend a seminar given by the International Association of Travel Agents, for which scholarships had been given. In a seperate incident, Cubana's Carmen Veiga and Rosa Pego denied visas to participate in an industry seminar.

Sugar officials Norge Bernal and Guillermo Alvarez denied visas to participate in an International workshop by the Society of Sugar Cane Specialists. Also, Rodolfo Maribona denied visa to attend an industry-related conference.

U.S. specialist Reinaldo González denied visa for a speaking tour hosted by the Venceremos Brigade, a U.S.-Cuba friendship society.

Luís Sandín Lazo de la Vega denied visa. The health official had been invited to the United States by the firm Siemens.

Athletic directors Rosa Escandell and Jesús Alvarez denied visas for a professional visit with their counterparts at the University of Wisconsin.

Ambassador Carlos Lechuga denied visa to participate at a roundtable discussion sponsored by Johns Hopkins University.

Orchestra Anacaona denied visas to perform at a New York music festival.

Drs. Manuel Cepero and Julio Díaz denied visas to attend an international surgery conference in Los Angeles.

Writer Armando Luís Fernandez denied visa for a professional visit with the Caribbean Studies Institute at the University of Puerto Rico.

Trainer Andres Luís Lobato denied visa to California for a U.S.-USSR boxing tournament.

January 1992 A number of public figures denied visas to address a Cuba solidarity rally in New York organized by the International Peace with Cuba Appeal and attended by some 4,000 people. Invitations had been extended to primarisima ballerina Alicia Alonso, boxer Teófilo Stevenson, historian Eusebio Leal, and performer Sara González.

February and September 1992 Two seperate times, three trade union leaders, Albis Nubia Favier Ramírez (Secretary General of the Union of Public Workers), Angel Luís Mena Kindelan (Secretary General of the Union of Light Industry Workers) and Manuel Montero (official of the Confederation of Cuban Trade

Unions) denied visas for a tour of 17 U.S. cities. They had been invited by the Detroit-based U.S.-Cuba Labor Exchange and the invitation had been issued by 16 U.S. trade union locals. In one protest note to the Cuba Desk at the Department of State, a trade union officer complains: "As U.S. citizens, we have the right to invite fellow trade unionists from other countries to visit us, to freely associate with whomever we choose, and to speak with whomever we choose. We just celebrated the 200th anniversary of the Bill of Rights. Is this the way the Bush Administration intends to honor it?"[59]

April 1992 Two women scientists denied visas to New York City where they were to begin work with the World Health Organization.

Methodist Bishop Joel Ajo is denied visa to attend his Church's International Bishop Conference in Lexington, Kentucky.

June 1992 Dr. Concepción Campa, the scientist who developed the world's first effective vaccine against meningitis type-B and director of Havana's Finlay Institute, denied visa to attend a conference at the National Centers for Disease Control in Atlanta, Georgia.

Maitre Laura Alonso and other instructors from Cuballet are denied visas to New York where they were going to teach classes; the workshops are instead held in Mexico and Sweden which followed their winter courses in Brazil and Argentina.

August 1992 Cuban cosmonaut, Arnaldo Tamayo Mendez, is denied visa to attend two scientific conferences in the U.S. capital. In a separate incident, three Cuban nuclear scientists denied visas to participate at a San Diego, California conference on peaceful nuclear development.

September 1992 Mayor of Havana Pedro Chávez denied visa to Detroit. He had been invited by the Detroit City Council whose president had visited Cuba last year.

Lawyers Elsa Agramonte and Tamara Colombia-Matos denied visa for a combined 50-city tour sponsored by the Cuba Women's Exchange. Invitations to the lawyers were issued by

---

[59] Letter dated February 7, 1992, addressed to Vicki Huddleston and signed by Robert T. Yeager, National Organization of Legal Services Workers.

some 16 colleges and universities including Vassar, the New School, Rutgers University, Harvard University, City College of New York, University of San Francisco, Northwestern University, and Duke University. The lawyers were also scheduled to address the 24th Convention of the National Conference of Black Lawyers.

1992 Set designers Mayda Bustamante and Jusé Forteza denied visas to Washington, D.C. where they planned to set the stage for an upcoming performance of the Cuba National Ballet at the John F. Kennedy Center.

Psychologist Marta Geóngora Ricardo denied visa to study at New York's National Institute for Emotional Therapy.

Support from all corners

"The pediatric medicines we are today donating to Cuba come from 32 states. Contributors to this effort tell us that they don't want to be associated with U.S. policy towards Cuba. So, the answer here is not humanitarian shipments but tearing down the blockade. "

Gloria Weinberg
U.S.+Cuba Medical Project
June 1992

Taking aim at the American eagle circling over Cuba are individuals and organizations who count their members in the millions, from Latin American heads of state and European parliamentarians to growing numbers in the United States at odds with the official trade ban. A 1992 public poll released by the Washington-based Commission on U.S.-Latin American relations found a majority of U.S. voters support a thaw in the Cold War in the Caribbean. A press release by the Commission asserts that:

> With the end of the Cold War, Americans no longer see Cuba as a security threat and are willing to consider closer ties to the Castro regime... Fewer than one in seven Americans now consider the overthrow of the Castro regime a top priority of U.S. policy.

Conducted by the Tarrance Group, traditionally aligned to the Republican Party, and Greenberg-Lake, pollsters for the Democratic Party, the bipartisan survey (with a 3.1 percent margin of error) learned that two-thirds of Democratic Party voters and three-quarters of Republicans say they are ready to put their differences with Cuba aside and let common sense prevail in U.S.-Cuban relations.

SURVEY HIGHLIGHTS

Should the United States re-establish diplomatic and economic relations with Cuba?

Yes	47%
No	41%
Unsure	12%

Do you favor President Bush's position that the United States will only improve relations with Cuba if there are free, multi-party elections, an end to human rights abuses, and a move to a market economy in Cuba?

Yes	70%
No	21%
Unsure	9%

How serious a threat is Cuba to U.S. security?

Not serious	67%
Serious	29%

Should the United States impose economic sanctions on countries that trade/invest in Cuba?

No	65%
Yes	19%
Unsure	15%

Should the United States abolish the travel ban?

Yes	53%
No	38%
Unsure	9%

Should the United States abolish the policy that bars phone and mail service to Cuba?

Yes	58%
No	30%
Unsure	12%

Straw polls among Cuban emigres living in the United States indicate that strong numbers oppose the blockade of food and medicines to the island. Two Miami-based organizations have garnered tens of thousands of signatures on petitions addressed to the U.S. Congress, calling for free trade of humanitarian goods between the United States and Cuba.[60] Concern for family deepened after direct phone service to the island went dead on August 23, 1992. Initially at fault was Hurricane Andrew which swept across the Florida peninsula and destroyed the tropospheric over-the-horizon radio link between the United States and Cuba: a public dial telephone service that may have been regarded as a breakthrough in communications back when it was installed in 1959 but dates "prehistoric" in the context of today's satellite age. What followed in the storm's wake proved more catastrophic to the phone link than Andrew's high winds and heavy rains: the U.S. embargo that keeps frozen the $80 million in 26 years of operating costs owed by AT&T to the Cuban phone company, Emtelcuba (thereby denying Cuba the capital to keep the phones ringing), and which prohibits Ma Bell from signing a standard operating agreement with its Cuban counterpart that would upgrade the system.

Normally, each phone company jointly handling an international call splits the customer charge. That is the arrangement AT&T has with every other communications provider in the world — except for Emtelcuba. According to Cuba's legal counsel, Michael Krinsky, for 30 years Cuban telephone operators have been essentially performing a free service by handling calls from the United States so that people were not cut off from family members living in the United States.[61] But a Cuban ministry of foreign relations statement issued September 7 explains that with today's economic crisis the island is in no financial position to "continue channeling our scarce resources in that direction." If not for the embargo, the solution is actually simple. Back in 1991, both phone companies agreed to activate an undersea telephone cable, stretching from West Palm

---

[60] The petition drive is being conducted by the Antonio Maceo Brigade and the Alliance of Cuban Workers. By December 1992, they expect they will have gathered over 60,000 signatures. During the Torricelli bill hearings in Spring 1992, representatives from the organizations flew to Washington to present a book-bound volume of the petitions to key Congressional members as stated opposition to the proposed legislation.

[61] Interview with author, September 11, 1992.

Beach to Havana that was installed in 1989. But the financial agreement between the two companies was never approved by U.S. Treasury and Cuba just doesn't have the cash to upgrade the link until it gets its fair share of the revenues.

Nothing better illustrates the spectrum of international opposition to the blockade than the tons of humanitarian aid pouring into the island from around the world, especially as it is a counterweight to renewed Bush administration lobbying for Cuba's isolation. Some may ask why Cuba, when there are dozens of countries in far worse shape? Organizers such as Domingo Chamorro, mayor of a small Spanish town that is sister city to Cuba's Los Palacios, believe that each donation of embargoed goods that safely arrives in Cuba constitutes a small chip in Washington's blockade.[62] Others feel that the Cubans, now in their hour of need, should reap the fruit of what they have sowed — having shared its doctors, engineers, and teachers with other developing countries for the last 30 years.

One poignant example sailed into the Havana harbor in late August 1992 aboard the Cuban vessel, the "Ignacio Agramonte." Its hulls — weighed down by $5 million worth of rice, spare parts and tires — had been loaded by the people and city council of the Spanish city Puerto Real. On receiving the donations, Havana's Mayor Pedro Chávez announced that the supplies would be used to keep basic services like ambulances and delivery trucks running in the capital. [63]

In just one four-month period in 1992, the following aid arrived on the island: 12 tons of medicines and hundreds of tons of clothing, food, tires and powdered milk collected by local government officials of Galicia, Spain; classroom supplies from grade school children in China; more school supplies and two buses from Tarragona municipality in Spain's Catalona region; a $10,000 check from Uruguay's "Dollar for Cuba" festival; a $3,600 check from supporters in India's southern state of Kerala and a promise from Indian farmers to send 82 tons of rice to the island; job safety equipment from Mexico's electrical workers union with more on the way; analgesics from Vietnam; sporting equipment, toys and medicines from the Ukrainian families of the children

---

[62] Radio Havana Cuba, May 8, 1992.

[63] Radio Havana Cuba, August 27, 1992.

receiving free medical care in Cuba for illness stemming from the Chernobyl nuclear accident; narcotic detection equipment from the British government; oil from Ecuador in a campaign spearheaded by Manuel Salgado, vice-president of the country's Congress, and other leading legislators; a shipload of medicines, construction materials, school supplies and a bicycle repair shop from Italy; medicines for a Havana maternity hospital from U.S. veterans working to normalize U.S.-Cuban relations; oil from Brazil; 4 tons of powdered milk and medicines from Argentina with a pledge to send oil-money to Cuba; a $17,000 donation from the Bolivian Confederation of Urban Teachers; a solidarity cargo of milk and medicines from a group of Valencian tourists; $70,000 worth of pediatric antibiotics from a U.S. medical aid project that asserts "The answer here is not humanitarian shipments... but tearing down the blockade"; $10,000 worth of paint and $200,000 worth of newsprint from the Basque country; and four tons of medicines worth $600,000 from Guadeloupe and Martinique, described by the Cuban press as "an impressive gesture of solidarity" considering that the combined population of the two islands is just 457,000 people. Through a narrow exception to the embargo law, some $100,000 worth of powdered milk, flour, canned meats, soap and medicines for AIDS patients was also sent from the U.S.-based National Council of Churches.[64]

---

[64] Various U.S. and Cuban press sources.

Voices from the international chorus calling for an end to the U.S. blockade against Cuba

"I call on this country to respect international law and self-determination, and to normalize relations with the Cubans. Surely, it is time to end the Cold War in this hemisphere. Let trade and travel grow."

Rev. Jesse Jackson
syndicated U.S. newspaper column
August 1992

(partial listing)
AFRICA
Angolan National Assembly
Joaquim Chissano, president of Mozambique
Kenneth Kaunda, former president of Zambia
Nelson Mandela, president of the African National Congress
Robert Mugabe, president of Zimbabwe
Sam Nujoma, president of Namibia
Julius Nyerere, former president of Tanzania
Organization of African Unity
Jose Eduardo dos Santos, president of Angola

ASIA
V.R.Krishna Iyer, chief justice of India, retired

Datuk Seri Mahathir, prime minister of Malaysia
Shaikh Mohammed Rashid, former deputy prime minister of
    Malaysia
Bishop Paulos Mar Paulos, Indian city of Cochin
Beant Singh, government minister of India

EUROPE
Tony Benn, member of British parliament
Julie Christie, actor
Jutta Ditfurth, former president of German Green Party
European Episcopal Conference
European Community (opposes "extraterritorial" application)
Group of 62 deputies of the European Parliament
Manuel Fraga, president of Spain's autonomous region of Galicia
George Galloway, member of British parliament
Italian Labor Confederation
Harry MacPherson, Longshoremen's Union, Scotland
Phil Manzanera, British musician
Methodist Church of Great Britain
Cardenal Angel Suquia, president of the Episcopal Conference
    of Spain and Archbishop of Madrid
Town of Los Palacios, Spain
Monique Picard-Weyl, Supreme Court, Paris
Roland Weyl, Supreme Court, Paris

LATIN AMERICA AND THE CARIBBEAN
Fabián Alarcón, president of Ecuador's National Congress
Clodomiro Almeyda, former foreign minister of Chile
Carlos Andres Pérez, president of Venezuela
Andean Parliament
Association of Latin American Jurists
Mario Benedetti, Uruguayan writer
Frei Betto, liberation theologian, Brazil
Leonardo Boff, liberation theologian, Brazil
Bolivian Teachers Confederation
Bolivian House of Representatives
Brazil's Senate of Federal Republic
Brazil's Workers Party
Humberto Calderon, Venezuela's foreign minister
Cuauhtemoc Cardenas, president of Mexico's second largest

political party, PDR
Caribbean Conference of Churches
Caribbean Council of Churches
Caribbean Federation of Youth
Church Councils of Canada, the Caribbean and Latin America
Fernando Collor de Mello, president of Brazil
Colombia's National Association of Exporters
COPPAL (Permanent Conference of Latin American Political
    Parties)
Council of Protestant Churches of Latin America and the
    Caribbean
Ecuadoran Parliament
Luiza Erundina de la Sousa, mayor of Sao Paolo, Brazil
Federation of Arab-American Organizations
Eduardo Galeano, Uruguayan author
Gabriel Garciá Márquez, writer
Cesar Gaviria, president of Colombia
Latin America and the Caribbean Christian Peace Conference
Latin American Council of Churches
Latin American Parliament
Latin American Human Rights Association
Latin American Region of World Federation of Trade Unions,
    representing 14 million members in 26 countries
Ignacio Lula da Silva, leader of Brazil's Workers Party
Miguel de la Madrid, former Mexican president
Dante Martins de Oliveira, former Brazilian minister
Methodist Church of the Caribbean and Latin America
Mexican Congress
Mexico's National Autonomous University
Mexico's National Federation of Lawyers
Nicaragua's Workers Federation (represents 65% of workforce)
Daniel Ortega, former president of Nicaragua
Panama's Evangelical Methodist Church
Panama's Federation of Public Employees Associations
Jaime Paz Zamora, president of Colombia
Adolfo Pérez Esquivel, Nobel Prize laureate
Peru's General Workers Confederation
Peru's House of Representatives
Peru's Senate
Puerto Rico's Federation of Teachers

Puerto Rico's National Ecumenical Movement
Carlos Salinas de Gortari, president of Mexico
Noemi Sanin, foreign minister of Colombia
Cardinal Angel Suquia, archbishop of Madrid
Trade Union Federation of the Southern Cone
Uruguay's National Congress of Mayors
Venezuela's Trade Union Federation, CUTV
Ruben Zamora, El Salvador

NORTH AMERICA

Brooke Adams, actor
African Methodist Church
American Association of Jurists
American Baptist Church
American Civil Liberties Union (opposes travel ban)
American Hotel and Motel Association
American Public Health Association
Antonio Maceo Brigade
Edward Asner, actor
Harry Belafonte, singer
Rev. Philip Berrigan
Rev. Oscar Bolioli, National Council of Churches
Jackson Browne, singer
Haywood Burns, National Conference of Black Lawyers
Bishop Charles A. Buswell
Zoe Caldwell, actor
Center for Constitutional Rights
Center for Cuban Studies
Professor Noam Chomsky, MIT
Christian Church, Disciples of Christ
Ramsey Clark, former U.S. attorney general
Dr. Johnnetta Cole, president of Spelman College
Irwin Corey, entertainer
Cuban American Coalition
Cuban American Health Professionals Association
John Conyers, Jr., member of Congress
Bishop Philip Cousin, African Methodist Church, U.S.
Angela Davis, former political prisoner, author, academic
Ossie Davis, actor
Ruby Dee, actor

Ron V. Dellums, member of Congress
Mervyn Dymally, member of Congress
Daniel Ellsberg
Episcopal Church
Evangelical Lutheran Church in America
Lawrence Ferlinghetti, poet
Henry González, member of Congress
Bishop Thomas J. Gumbleton
Richie Havens, singer
Lennox Hinds, Esq
Hispanic American Political Association
International Association of Journalists, U.S. chapter
Rev. Jesse Jackson
Casey Kasem, radio broadcaster
Margot Kidder, actor
Michael Krinsky, Esq
Kris Kristofferson, singer and actor
William Kunstler, Esq
Latin American Studies Association
Cindi Lauper, singer
Bishop Rev. Edward L. Lee, Jr.
Jack Lemmon, actor
Ken Lerch, president, National Association of Letter Carriers
Bishop Raymond A. Lucker
Madison, Wisconsin City Council
Norman Mailer, author
Cheech Marin, actor
Paul Mazursky, film director and producer
George McGovern, former senator
Kate Millet, writer
Robert McNamara, former U.S. secretary of defense
Bishop Paul Moore, Jr.
Dave Nagle, member of Congress
National Conference of Black Lawyers
National Conference of Catholic Bishops
National Council of Churches of Canada
National Council of Churches of Christ
National Lawyers Guild
Holly Near, singer and songwriter
Pastors for Peace

Linus Pauling, Nobel Prize laureate
Pax World Foundation
Gregory Peck, actor and producer
Sydney Pollack, film director and producer
Bishop Kenneth Povish
Presbyterian Church
John Randolph, actor
Charles Rangel, member of Congress
Michael Ratner, Esq.
Cleveland Robinson, United Auto Workers/District 65
Susan Sarandon, actor
Gus Savage, member of Congress
Bishop Walter J. Schoenherr
Pete Seeger, singer and songwriter
Martin Sheen, actor
Wayne S. Smith, former head of U.S. Interests Section in Havana
Bishop Walter F. Sullivan
Benjamin Spock, MD
Studs Terkel, author
Unitarian Universalist Association of Congregations
United Church of Canada
United Church of Christ
United Methodist Church
United Presbyterian Church
United States Businessmen's Conference
Veterans for Peace, U.S. chapter
Prof. George Wald, Nobel Prize laureate
Alice Walker, writer
Maxine Waters, member of Congress
William Winpisinger, International Association of Machinists
Workers' Association of the Cuban Community, Miami
Peter Yarrow, singer

INTERNATIONAL
Nonaligned Nations Movement
World Alliance of Reformed Churches
World Council of Churches
World Federation of Trade Unions

"It's incredibly immoral"

"The blockade? It's impact on our school is even worse today. We can't afford to go half-way around the world for finger paints, crayons or modeling clay — when it is work just to make sure that there is enough protein for the children's hot lunches. Milk is our number one priority. And to ensure enough for every kid, we have limited enrollment to infants over 6 months. This, in turn, affects working mothers who are nursing. They not only have to find someone to watch their babies but also figure out how to continue nursing on the job. The blockade is a nightmare!"

Virginia Ramírez
"Lindos Pececitos" Day Care Center
Cayo Hueso, Havana

"It was the community's decision to name our day care center after Samantha Smith... we were all moved by how this child came to profoundly understand the need for peace, what peace means for the children of the world. To be able to live in peace, to run and play and share — no matter where they come from. From Cuba. From the United States. From all of the Americas. A child who seemed to know better than her own government which devotes its time to taking milk away from our toddlers instead of reaching out to help them grow strong. This is why Samantha is alive in the hearts of our children."

Delia Granados
"Samantha Smith" Day Care Center
Santiago de las Vegas, Cuba

"During World War II, Cuba implemented a ration system. When the war was over, so was food rationing. We began rationing again in 1962. Why? Because we are at war again. A war that unfortunately hasn't ended. The long struggle against the blockade goes on, and the ration system is a way of guaranteeing the basics for everyone."
Mirta Muñiz
retired advertising woman

"...I really believe that health should be independent of politics. I'm sure that if we invented some medicine that would cure AIDS, we would sell it to every country in the world — without exception. We wouldn't blockade it. That's basic morality!"
José Antonio
33-year old Cuban hemophiliac
who has died of AIDS

"Some AIDS patients can't eat solid food, because this virus attacks the proteins of the body. We need protein supplements and they have those pills in the United States. But we can't get them, except through third or fourth countries. Just like the drugs DDI and AZT. We have trouble getting those medicines from the United States too."
A 50-year old Cuban man infected with AIDS. He died from
stomach cancer six weeks after the interview.

"It's estimated that over the last 30 years, some 30 million U.S. tourists would have visited Cuba if it had not been for the blockade. If we calculate this in terms of 1959 profits, the island lost some $3.5 billion."
Nicanor Leon Cotayo
author of *Beleaguered Hope*

"It's incredibly immoral to play politics with food and medicine."
Dr. Jaime Bernaza
kidney transplant surgeon for 20 years

"During 40 years of apartheid in South Africa, the United States never managed to fully comply with the sanctions, with the economic blockade, against the white racists in Pretoria. They bought and sold, and profited, while Black South Africa pleaded and demanded they stop. The tactic of economic blockade was reserved as a punishment for Cuba. We — like a democratic, non-racial South Africa — are apparently the real threat to the U.S. government."
Carmen González, historian
author of *U.S. Policy for Southern Africa*

"The U.S. blockade is certainly making AIDS a more dangerous disease for Cubans... One example: condoms are imported in hard currency. It's a simple thing but for millions of people, this means that the blockade has once again become a life or death matter... Another case is AZT. The United States has refused to allow us to buy AZT and has prevented laboratories in other countries from selling it to Cuba. That's a direct attack on AIDS patients and a terrible violation of their right to fight for their lives."
sociologist Manuel Hernández
National AIDS Education Campaign

"I feel the blockade every day — starting at 5 a.m. when I have to get up to take the bus since there are few buses because of the fuel shortage. We are managing to give the school kids books, pads and pencils, but we're running out. And teaching aids are scarce so we're inventing our own. So, I feel the blockade every day and every day I ask myself "why?" What could possibly justify such a bitter inhuman policy against children?"
Rosa Idalia Hernández
primary school teacher
Central Havana

Resolutions demanding an end to the blockade

CUBAN ECUMENICAL COUNCIL
resolution adopted September 4, 1991
Blessed are the Peacemakers, for they shall be called the children of God.

Matthew 5:9

We Christians have been discovering the hand of God in the origins of time; He is guiding individuals, peoples and institutions towards the realization of His will, and God's will is that we should all take part in His Kingdom, which is justice, love and peace.

The Cuban Ecumenical Council, an organization uniting churches and institutions which are working for peace and love among people, cannot remain detached in the face of injustice and enmity.

For these reasons, as Christians among the Cuban people, we note with great satisfaction that our government's representative to the United Nations, Mr. Ricardo Alarcón de Quesada, has proposed that the question of the embargo against Cuba be considered by the General Assembly at this session.

We cannot be indifferent to the unjust economic embargo against Cuba, since it has meant that the people have had to pay a high price for these past 30 years and more.

Because it disregards the supreme dignity of all people, because of its degrading implications for health, the well-being and development and because it violates the right of every human being to life itself, we address ourselves to you, asking that you heed our plea, as Christians and as Cubans, so that we be allowed to determine our future in a free and sovereign manner.

We believe that there are inviolable principles which

identify us as Christians, compelling us to reject the commercial embargo imposed on our country; we know that God will place in your mind and heart the will to ensure that justice shines forth for the good of all our people, and we hope that this question will be considered at the forthcoming session of the General Assembly.

REGIONAL METHODIST CHURCHES
adopted on August 16, 1991
On August 14, 1991, in Antigua, Guatemala, the Council of Bishops of the Council of Methodist Churches in Latin America and the Caribbean signed a declaration in support of the people of Cuba.

In solidarity with the Cuban people, and endorsing the terms of the above-mentioned declaration, the Meeting of Methodist Churches held in Antigua, Guatemala, calls for:

1. An end to the unjust and prolonged blockade against Cuba, promoted by the United States of America, which is affecting the lives of our Cuban brothers.
2. The support of all the countries of the Americas and the Caribbean for the people of Cuba, so that they may freely and wisely determine their destiny, without pressure or threats of intervention.

Bishop Etchegoyen
Council of Methodist Churches in the Caribbean and the Americas
Rev. C. Evans Bailey
Methodist Church in Latin America and the Caribbean
Bishop Melvin Talvert
United Methodist Church of United States
Mrs. Rosemary Wass
Methodist Church of Great Britain
Rev. Tom Edmonds
United Church of Canada

LATIN AMERICAN PARLIAMENT RESOLUTION
passed August 2, 1991 and reaffirmed May 19, 1992
The 13th Regular General Assembly of the Latin American Parliament, meeting in Cartagena, Colombia, from July 31 to

August 3, 1991, has agreed on the following:

1. Noting with concern that for the last 30 years the sister people of Cuba have been suffering under a rigid economic and trade blockade, which even applies to food and medicine;

2. Deeply concerned by the fact that the blockade of Cuba has caused serious difficulties for that nation's economy, consequently detrimental to the entire population;

3. Considering that this kind of practice, in addition to violating international law, goes against the spirit that prevails in today's world, characterized by detente, the relaxing of cold war tensions and greater understanding between the great powers, which propitiates the process of democratization in all regions of the globe; we resolve,

1. To express our solidarity with the people of Cuba, in the face of the serious economic situation that they are now facing;

2. To ask for an end to the economic and trade blockade imposed on that island for 30 years.

LATIN AMERICAN PARLIAMENT
Submitted May 19, 1992 to the UN secretary-general

The Permanent Committee on Health, Labour and Social Security of the Latin American Parliament, based in Havana, Cuba, meeting from March 24 to 27, 1992 and attended by 75 parliamentarians from Argentina, Bolivia, Brazil, Chile, Colombia, Cuba, the Dominican Republic, Ecuador, Guatemala, Honduras, Mexico, the Netherlands Antilles, Panama, Paraguay, Peru, Uruguay and Venezuela, considering:

1. that the international community recognizes, as basic principles of peaceful coexistence among States, the self-determination of peoples and non-intervention in their sovereign decisions,

2. that for 34 years the Cuban people have been undergoing a process of transformation in which the efforts of its workers have brought it considerable economic and social progress,

3. that the Republic of Cuba has achieved fundamental advances for its people in living and health standards, as well as in social security, that malnutrition and illiteracy have been eradicated, and that the levels of life expectancy and of child and maternal mortality are equal to the best recorded in the developed countries, all of which sets an example for the

majority of our nations,

4. that a criminal blockade against Cuba is being maintained and intensified, in disregard of international principles, aggravating the difficulties under which the Cuban people currently live and further hampering the effort to maintain its economic and social achievements,

therefore agrees:

1. to congratulate the Government and people of the Republic of Cuba on their major achievements in the fields of health, labor and social security, encouraging them to persist in their efforts to promote development and social progress;

2. to express our appreciation to the Government and people of Cuba for their action in solidarity with our peoples and their commitment to Latin American integration;

3. to condemn the blockade against the Republic of Cuba and call for its cessation, and to urge the Latin American Parliament to make these demands both at the Organization of American States and at the United Nations.

LETTER TO THE UNITED NATIONS SECRETARY-GENERAL
Signed by 70 patients in a Havana hospital on March 23, 1992
We, the undersigned, patients who have been treated in Havana's "Frank Pais" Orthopedic Hospital, together with our families, wish to express our feelings of solidarity and gratitude for everything that we have received.

We will leave Cuba with not just our health and the joy of being cured, but also with a lesson about life, a lesson which many of us learned during the long period of time we spent with the men, women and children of this country. We have been convinced once again that the embargo, which has been imposed on the Cuban people and causes suffering and hardship, is unjust and inhumane.

We are therefore writing to you to request that the embargo be lifted so that this united, deserving and generous people are allowed to live in peace, and allowed to work and struggle as they choose and have done so over the years.

Patients from Argentina, Benin, Bolivia, Colombia, Dominican Republic, Ecuador, Guyana, Mexico, Nicaragua, Palestine, Panama, Peru, Spain, Uruguay, and Venezuela.

TRADE UNION FEDERATIONS OF THE SOUTHERN CONE
March 12, 1992

The Trade Union Federations of the Southern Cone, whose signatures appear below, met in Sao Paulo during the month of March 1992, and declared the urgent necessity of ending the economic blockade imposed on Cuba for more than 30 years.

We declare that the self determination of all of Latin America's people be unequivocally respected as it ought to be throughout the world.

CGT, Argentina	COB, Bolivia
CUT, Brazil	CUT , Chile
CUT, Paraguay	PIT/CNT, Uruguay

PUERTO RICAN TEACHERS' FEDERATION

Whereas, since 1961, the United States, as part of its aggressive policy against Cuba, has applied an economic, commercial and financial blockade for the purpose of imposing a political, social and economic order more acceptable to U.S. authorities.

Whereas, the objective of the U.S. government is to ruin the Cuban economy and impede that people's exercise of their right to self-determination, independence and sovereignty.

Whereas, the blockade has affected the entire Cuban people who through tremendous vigor and sacrifice work and struggle to develop their nation.

Whereas, the blockade of the United States, in open violation of all civil and human rights, has barred Cuba's access to food, medicine and medical equipment produced in the United States.

Whereas, this criminal practice, totally and systematically applied over three decades, has caused (and continues to cause) visible damage to the Cuban people.

Whereas the interdependency of the people of the world is a reality that must be respected especially by those countries which speak about democracy.

Whereas, the evident social gains achieved by the Cuban nation — one of which is the educational system and other achievements linked to the welfare of Cuba's children and youth — are being adversely affected by the blockade and other actions on the part of the United States.

Whereas, as Puerto Rican educators, we have the duty to demonstrate our solidarity with every effort to stop political or other types of actions that deprive a people of their self-determination and culture.

Whereas, we recognize the historic links between our two peoples.

Therefore be it resolved by this assembly of delegates to the Puerto Rican Teachers' Federation meeting September 29, 1991 on Green Island that:

1. we repudiate the economic aggression against the Cuban people;

2. we demand that the U.S. government end its economic aggression against Cuba which violates the Cuban people's most fundamental human rights;

3. we demand that the UN General Assembly protect the rights of all people to self-determination, independence and sovereignty, and put an end to this unjust, illegal and immoral situation which is an offense to all Latin Americans.

4. a copy of this resolution be made public...

5. this resolution be sent to the Secretary-General of the United Nations, the Cuban Women's Federation and the Cuban Teachers Union.

CITY COUNCIL OF MADISON, WISCONSIN
March 17, 1992

Whereas, February 3, 1992 marked the 30th year of the United States' economic embargo against Cuba which ended all economic and financial ties between the two countries including medicine and food; and

Whereas, the United States travel ban to Cuba has restricted our own citizens' ability to travel, study or visit relatives in Cuba and has eliminated intellectual, cultural and scientific exchange; and

Whereas, the continuation of the economic embargo is causing the people of Cuba underserved hardship; and

Whereas, the government of Cuba has withdrawn its military forces from Africa and renounced support for armed struggle in this hemisphere, conditions set forth by the United States for lifting the embargo; and

Whereas, the support and relationship between the

government of Cuba and the former "Eastern Bloc" nations has ended, as has the "Cold War"; and

Whereas, the United States economic embargo and travel ban against Cuba has separated families, isolated citizens of both countries and ended free trade;

Now, therefore, be it resolved, that the City of Madison calls for the normalization of diplomatic and economic relations with Cuba; and

Be it further resolved, that we call for an end to the United States' intervention in the internal affairs of Cuba, such as Radio and TV Martí; and

Be it finally resolved, that the City of Madison urges passage of HR 434, introduced by Congressman Ted Weiss of New York, to create an exemption to the Trade Embargo allowing the export of medical supplies and equipment to Cuba, and passage as well of the Free Trade in Ideas Act, which would allow United States citizens to travel to Cuba.

Tracking the Torricelli Bill

After months of redrafting the "Cuban Democracy Act of 1992," Rep. Robert Torricelli [D-NJ] introduced the proposed legislation on February 5, 1992 at a press conference where he shared the limelight with Jorge Mas Canosa, president of the Cuban American National Foundation who participated in the April 1961 Bay of Pigs invasion. As chair of the Western Hemisphere subcommittee of the Democratic Party-controlled House Foreign Affairs Committee, Torricelli issued a challenge to the Republican White House to update its Cuba policy. Cuba-bashing became a recurrent theme in the election year, principally to undermine Bush's perceived foreign policy achievements and vie for contributions from the wealthy wing of the Cuban-American community. The Torricelli bill seeks to extend and tighten the U.S. imposed embargo against Cuba. Among its many features, the bill includes:

— the language of the Mack Amendment, which would end U.S. corporate subsidiary trade with Cuba (70 percent of which is in foods and medicines);
— calling on the president to pressure Western allies to enforce the embargo;
— sanctioning Latin American countries that trade with Cuba;
— stopping any ship that trades at a Cuban port from trading at a U.S. port for the following six months;
— U.S. government funding and supplying of opposition groups on and off the island.

The bill is further complicated by the inclusion of items which would seem to improve phone and mail service between Cuba and the United States. Since the bill does not address some of the

outstanding issues between the two countries on these points —
namely authorizing AT&T to settle its $80 million debt with the
Havana phone company — observers believe that the language
was put there more for marketing purposes within the United
States.

Once introduced, the bill was quickly sent to six committees of
the House of Representatives: Foreign Affairs; Energy and
Commerce; Merchant Marine and Fisheries; Ways and Means;
Post Office and Civil Service; and, Banking, Finance and Urban
Affairs. Upon learning that senior lawmakers on Banking
planned to squash the initiative, Torricelli scratched a number of
clauses that removed it from their jurisdiction.

On March 18, the House Foreign Affairs Committee convened
the first of what would be three public hearings on the "Cuban
Democracy Act of 1992." In perhaps one of the most telling
moments in this whole process, the proceedings were delayed
several hours when Mas Canosa's private jet from Florida was
late arriving. He, along with elected officials and State
Department representatives, gave testimony at that first
hearing.

According to information on record with the Federal Election
Commission, Torricelli's largest financial backer is the "Free
Cuba" Political Action Committee, which is directly tied to Mas
Canosa and the Cuban American National Foundation. With his
hands in one of the biggest campaign chests in the House of
Representatives, Torricelli denies any connection between
donations from right-wing Cuban-Americans and his decision to
introduce his embargo-tightening bill. Yet in the four years before
Torricelli took over the Western Hemisphere subcommittee he
received less than $2,000 from the "Free Cuba" PAC. Soon after
that figure jumped to the maximum $10,000 contribution, Rep.
Torricelli introduced his bill. He was also handed an additional
$16,750 from individual wealthy Cuban-Americans such as Mas
Canosa and his wife.

On May 21, the Foreign Affairs Committee of the House met
to vote on the bill, having completed its hearings. Before the
final verdict was in, Rep. Ted Weiss [D-NY] introduced an
amendment exempting medicines, medical supplies and
equipment from the U.S. embargo. Surprising everyone, the
amendment passed (11 to 10). Reading the writing on the wall,

Torricelli quickly adjourned the meeting and reconvened it two weeks later when ready with new ammunition.

Torricelli opened the June 4 session with a new clause to undercut Weiss' humanitarian gesture, knowing that what he would be demanding of the Cubans would be soundly rejected by any country. Tagged on is the mandate that a U.S. government official is to accompany every shipment of a U.S. medicine sale to the island in order to oversee the distribution of those goods. After the amendment passed, Weiss tried once more to exempt food from the embargo. This time, with the cards stacked in Torricelli's favor, that gesture was defeated and within 24 hours the Committee had approved the entire Act. Over the next few months, without even bothering to hold hearings on the bill, the Merchant Marine and Fisheries Committee, Energy and Commerce, and Post Office and Civil Service affixed their seals of approval to the bill, with the last two committees waving their jurisdiction over the legislation. On September 10, the Act cleared the hurdle of the Trade subcommittee of the House Ways and Means Committee, sending it to the full finance body.

The real blockade action came from the Senate side of the Congress. As controversial propositions sometimes do, the Torricelli bill snuck to the Oval Office through a back door. First, Senator Bob Graham unveiled the bill in his chamber at the same time that Torricelli did so in the House. The Committee on Foreign Relations waited until August before its Western Hemisphere subcommittee held a hearing and did little else until two weeks before the senators adjourned to hit the campaign trail. At that time Graham made the entire bill a footnote to the Defense Appropriations Act — which had already been approved by the House minus the blockade-tightening measures. Without ever holding a full debate in the House, Torricelli and his Florida ally managed to shoot the bill straight to the president's desk. It should be noted that in the 10-month legislative process, Torricelli repeatedly refused to meet with voters from his district opposed to the act and his friendship with the Cuban American National Foundation.

The following excerpts from testimony before the various committee hearings reflect the substance of the opposition to the "Cuban Democracy Act of 1992."

VICTOR SIDEL, MD, ON BEHALF OF THE AMERICAN
PUBLIC HEALTH ASSOCIATION

...I am a physician and am currently Distinguished University Professor in Social Medicine at Montefiore Medical College and the Albert Einstein College of Medicine in the Bronx, New York. I am a past President of APHA and a member of its Governing Council. I also represent the Public Health Association of New York City, of which I am also a past president. In addition , I am a past president of Physicians for Social Responsibility and its representative on the International Council of the International Physicians for the Prevention of Nuclear War, recipient of the 1985 Nobel Peace Prize.

APHA, representing a combined national and state affiliate membership of over 50,000 public health professionals and community leaders, has a long record of advocacy in support of improved health of people in the United States and around the world. In 1977, APHA adopted a resolution opposing the U.S. trade embargo on Cuba and calling for its immediate termination. This resolution notes that "this unilateral blockade violates principles of international cooperation, blocks negotiations to resolve remaining differences between Cuba and the United States, and limits the access of the United States public to information about Cuba, including information on Cuba's accomplishment in public health." The resolution further notes that the "prohibition on medical supplies specifically violates long-standing principles of international relations and fundamental concerns for human rights, and represents an attempted attack on the health and well-being of an entire population." This resolution stands today as one of the priority statements of APHA's concern that the health of the Cuban people is not held hostage to U.S. foreign policy considerations.

As the APHA resolution indicates, the current embargo obstructs the flow of information to the U.S. public about conditions in Cuba. Last January, members of the APHA Executive Board travelled to Cuba for eight days to get a first-hand impression of their public health system. While the members of the Board were guests of the government of Cuba and were accompanied by ministry of health officials during much of the visit, the Board members all felt that they were able to learn a great deal about health in Cuba. They were all struck by the wide gap between what they had expected to find and the true situation in the country.

...Cuba's accomplishments over the past 30 years are substantial in health, education and the eradication of extreme poverty. Through a complete restructuring of its health care system, Cuba has developed an exemplary national health system, which provides comprehensive, accessible health care to the entire population free of charge. Health facilities and personnel have been greatly expanded despite the exodus to the United States of many doctors and other trained personnel after Castro took power in 1959. Rural and mountainous areas of the country which had practically no access to health services prior to the revolution are now covered. The striking inequalities in the distribution of doctors, hospitals, and other health resources that existed before the revolution have been erased. The emphasis has shifted from treatment services for the few to health prevention and promotion for the entire population.

Cuba also embarked on an effort to advance medical science and available health care services to levels now matched only in the world's richest countries. Tertiary (highly specialized) care utilizes the latest in diagnostic and treatment techniques — including ultrasound, CAT scan, nuclear magnetic resonance, organ transplant, in-vitro fertilization, prenatal diagnosis of congenital defects, and neonatal care. The members of the Board visited many of these research and specialized care centers during their visit, and could not help but be deeply impressed with the unprecedented achievements of a developing country.

These efforts are reflected in the impressive health indicators Cuba has achieved over the past three decades. Two of the indicators used most by the United Nations specialized agencies such as the World Health Organization and Unicef to assess a country's overall health status are the infant mortality rate and the under-5 child mortality rate. According to the most recent data published by Unicef, Cuba ranks 25th in the world for both indicators, ahead of all other Latin America countries — indeed, ahead of all developing countries. The United States ranks 20th in the world for both indicators.

Cuba's infant mortality rate declined from 62 in 1960 to 11 in 1990, and the under-5 mortality rate improved from 87 in 1960 to 14 in 1990. While Cuba in 1960 was already ahead of most other

Third World countries in health indicators, these further declines in mortality are the most difficult to achieve. The two other countries in Latin America which had 1960 rates similar to Cuba's, have not achieved the advances made by Cuba. Argentina, which began in 1960 with infant and under-5 mortality rates respectively of 61 and 75, only advanced to 31 and 35 in 1990. Uruguay advanced from 51 and 57 to 22 and 25. These comparisons, along with data for the United States and Japan — the world's leaders in health indicators — show that Cuba's accomplishments are very real.

	Infant mortality rate		Under-5 mortality rate	
	1960	1990	1960	1990
Cuba	62	11	87	14
Argentina	61	31	75	35
Uruguay	51	22	57	25
USA	26	09	29	11
Japan	31	05	39	06

These advances have been made, and maintained, in spite of Cuba having a per-capita GNP in 1989 of about one-half that of Argentina and Uruguay and one-twentieth that of the United States and Japan. Even in the worse of economic times, Cuba has consistently made health a top priority and has allocated the funds necessary to maintain the health systems.

Today, however, Cuba's advances in health are in danger of being reversed, due in large part to the current crisis resulting from the termination of the Soviet economic subsidy. However, S.2918, if passed, will undoubtedly contribute to a deterioration in the health of the Cuban people. In particular, S.2918's interference in the Cuban people's access to food and medicine is tantamount to the use of food and medicine as a weapon in the U.S. arsenal against Cuba.

The bill's restrictions on trade with Cuba by subsidiaries of U.S. companies blocks the sale of food and medicines, which have comprised about 70 percent of that subsidiary trade. The sanctions of ships entering Cuba are another deterrent to the delivery of food and medicines to that country. The condition imposed on the sale of medicines and medical equipment to Cuba that the U.S. government verify their end-use through on-site inspection violates the concept of patient privacy and infringes on the country's national sovereignty. The requirement effectively blocks sales of medicines and medical equipment to Cuba, as that country will certainly reject any such on-site inspections.

In addition, restrictions on travel and communication contained in S.2918 prevent effective exchange of information on public health issues and other important matters. Health professionals in the United States have much to learn from our colleagues in Cuba regarding protecting the health of our people, just as health professionals in Cuba can benefit from unrestricted contacts from colleagues in the United States. The bill introduced in the House by Representative Howard Berman (H.R. 5406, the "Free Trade in Ideas" Act) would lift these restrictions on travel and information exchange, and represents a step towards a more enlightened policy rather than continuing with the same isolationist policy of the past.

APHA does not agree with all aspects of Cuban health policy. We have serious questions about the efficacy and ethics of the policy of restricting persons with HIV or AIDS to a sanitarium. In 1987, APHA passed a resolution opposing "the imposition of restrictions on the basic liberties or activities of people in the absence of scientific evidence that such measures will protect public health." Should the allegations of abuse of psychiatric facilities and resources be true, clearly we would oppose any such violations of human rights. Whatever the validity of any allegations regarding the Cuban health care system, however, it would in no way validate a policy of withholding food and medicines from the population.

In some circumstances, the use of economic sanctions may well be appropriate and effective policy tools. In 1981 the International Conference on Apartheid and Health, sponsored by the World Health Organization, called on the international community to sever trade links with South Africa. APHA supported that recommendation. However, in the case of South Africa, this was a policy that enjoyed wide international support, and it did not hinder the people's access to food and medicine. APHA's position is that measures that hinder the flow of food, medicines, and other resources essential to human survival should never be taken, no matter how laudable the ultimate goals may be. Invariably, the ones to suffer the greatest are the most vulnerable sectors of the population: very young children, the elderly and the sick.

We respectfully urge you to reconsider this effort to bring change to Cuba through a heavy-handed and destructive embargo. Surely in this day, with the Cold War behind us, the most powerful nation in the world can devise a policy that does not cause suffering among an entire population in order to accomplish our national political objectives.

More could be accomplished for the people of Cuba and for the people of the United States through a positive approach that includes lifting the embargo and encouraging a broad exchange of medical, scientific, and technical information and personnel.

REPRESENTATIVE DAVE NAGEL (D-IOWA)
... I strongly support a U.S. policy that fosters change in Cuba, but embargoes are not policies in and of themselves, they are instruments of foreign policy... we should exempt all food and medicines from the embargo, lift the restrictions on travel and take a closer look at the political impact that economic reform may have on Cuba's political system.

From a humanitarian standpoint, the United States has a long tradition of excluding medicines and food from embargoes, even in time of armed conflict. During the most severe freezes of the Cold War, many of my constituents in Iowa were allowed to sell their grain to the Soviet Union. More recently, one need only compare the UN sanctions on Iraq with those applied to Cuba to realize a vastly different standard is being applied. As a matter of principle and national policy, I think our policy is wrong — the United States should not be in the business of preventing people access, regardless of their country's government, to food and medicines.

HR 4168 would limit the availability of food and medicines for the Cuban population by restricting U.S. subsidiary trade with Cuba [the Mack Amendment]. Mr. Chairman, I would like to introduce for the record a July 1991 Special Report published by the Office of Foreign Assets Control of the Treasury Department... the report demonstrates an increase of over $300 million of exports to Cuba by U.S. subsidiary companies in 1990 — more than

90 percent of these exports were in grains, wheats and other consumables. On the other hand, Cuban sales to U.S. subsidiaries have not increased; therefore, the greatest impact of this provision of the bill will be on the availability of these products in Cuba while not having a great impact on Cuban exports.

Furthermore, this aspect of the bill along with other provisions could have a serious impact on our foreign relations with those countries affected by the legislation. Canada and England have already passed legislation to block the effects of the Mack Amendment (HR 4168)... The sanctions on governments that provided "assistance" to Cuba, according to the definition of "assistance" provided in the bill, would apparently affect a number of Latin American countries. Several normal trade practices are included in this definition: guarantees, insurance and tariff agreements, for example... In practice, how could we enforce this legislation? Do we plan to set up a U.S. government review process of trade agreements between our allies and Cuba?... I would argue from a practical standpoint, not only will our allies not abide by the provisions of this bill, but that American companies will be left behind — locking out American producers of foods and medicines while their European, Canadian and Latin American competitors establish a foothold...

"Recent measures by the United States to reinforce the illegal economic, commercial and financial blockade against Cuba"

Presented to the United Nations General Assembly on
August 26, 1992 by the Permanent Mission of Cuba

On April 24, 1992, the United States closed its ports to all third-country vessels "carrying goods or passengers to or from Cuba" (57 Federal Register 15216. April 24, 1992). By thus disrupting natural shipping routes and driving up freight costs, the United States seeks to discourage Cuba's export of its products and its import of third-country products.

Not content, the United States extended this new prohibition to third-country vessels carrying goods in which Cuba has any "interest." Cuba is deemed to have an "interest" in goods owned by third-country companies if they are made or derived in whole or in part of any article which is the growth, produce or manufacture of Cuba. Thus, for example, a third-country vessel could not put into a United States port if it was carrying from one third country to another steel products manufactured by a third-country company with trace amounts of Cuban-origin nickel or third-country food products processed with Cuban-origin sugar. With this prohibition, the United States seeks to discourage third-country companies from purchasing Cuban-origin articles for use in the manufacture of their own exports.

To underscore their importance, the president of the United States personally announced these new administrative measures (statement of the President, the White House, Office of the Press Secretary Kennebunkport, Maine, April 18, 1992). Far from exhibiting any appreciation of the constraints on international law and comity, the United States president brazenly proclaimed the United States intention "to isolate Cuba" until it abandons its internal political institutions in favour of those more to the liking of the United States. In a subsequent statement (letter of June 4, 1992) to Congress, the United States president, with equal disregard for international law and comity, proclaimed that these measures are "meant to discourage countries from increasing trade with Cuba and limit the development of tourism." There is no pretense whatsoever that the closing of United States ports to third-country vessels, or the avowed United States "policy of economic and political isolation" of which it is a part, is in response to any activity of Cuba in the international sphere or is in any way related to the security interests of the United States.

At the same time, the United States president endorsed the legislative initiative to close U.S. ports to third-country vessels for 180 days after they trade in a Cuban port without regard to the origin or destination of the cargo on board. Thus, for example, a third-country vessel that offloads cargo in Cuba and takes nothing on board could not enter a United States port for 180 days. The same would be true for a third-country vessel that takes on cargo in Havana and delivers it in a third country (testimony of State Department representative David Dworkin, hearings on the "Cuban Democracy Act of 1992," HR 5322, House Foreign Affairs Committee, May 28, 1992).

The international community has already condemned these actions as being in derogation of third-country rights and interests. In a memorandum circulated in the United States Congress, the European Community wrote of the April 18 administrative measures now in effect:

> These regulations are in conflict with long-standing rules on comity and international shipping and will adversely affect the European Community's trade with the United States.

Referring both to the April 18 administrative measures and the

United States president's endorsement of the shipping provision in the Cuban Democracy Act, the European Community wrote further:

> We are concerned at the apparent willingness of the United States government to endorse passage of a Cuban Democracy Act containing extraterritorial elements which will disrupt the normal business activities of companies and shipping lines based in Member States of the European Community. These measures would constitute the second batch of actions (following the Treasury regulations referred to above) which would be aimed at forcing foreign persons outside the proper jurisdiction of the United States to submit to United States law and foreign policy. As we have reiterated on countless occasions, such extraterritorial extension of the United States jurisdiction is unacceptable as a matter of law and policy... We hope that the United States Administration and Congress will reflect further on the expediency of supporting legislation which has the capacity to cause damage to trade relations at a time when the bilateral and multilateral agenda is already overcharged. Recognition by allied countries of different economic and foreign policy approaches to countries should be a normal result of international discourse between them. Attempts to force one country's agenda on the other can only lead to conflict and to a denial of the principles that the European Community-United States Transatlantic Declaration is designed to underpin.

Earlier, in response to a similar proposal then pending in the United States Congress to close U.S. ports, the European Community had stressed that the proposal, "which even in war time would be an infringement of the international law on neutral shipping, is completely unacceptable in peace time," (*Démarche*, April 18, 1990), and "would be in conflict with long-standing rules on comity and international law" (*Démarche*, April 7, 1992).

What was said with respect to the United States infringing upon the rights and interests of the European Community is of course equally true with respect to the rights and interests of all Member States of the United Nations.

Even the United States previously recognized that the

shipping measures it has now adopted would violate the rights of third countries. In 1975, the Organization of American States (OAS) lifted its collective sanctions against Cuba and resolved "to leave the State parties to the Rio Treaty free to normalize or conduct in accordance with the national policy and interests of each their relations with the Republic of Cuba at the level and in the form that each State deems advisable" (Final Act of the 16th Meeting of Consultation of Ministers of Foreign Affairs, OAS/Ser.F/11.16, Doc. 9/75 rev.2, July 29, 1975). The United States expressly recognized that "in order to conform" with this action of the OAS it was necessary for it to repeal those aspects of its economic blockade which penalized third-country vessels that trade with Cuba (Department of State Bulletin 404 [1975]). Accordingly, "in keeping with this action by the OAS," the United States repealed its long-standing prohibition against the bunkering of third-country vessels engaged in trade with Cuba (40 Federal Register 171, p. 10,508 [September 3, 1975]). The measure adopted now is even more extreme than that which, in 1975, the United States acknowledged would violate the rights of third countries in the absence of collective sanctions, since it denies entry to United States ports altogether and not merely bunkering privileges. As stated in the Declaration on Principles of International Law concerning Friendly Relations and Cooperation among States in accordance with the Charter of the United Nations, adopted in 1970 by the General Assembly without dissent:

> No State or group of States has the right to intervene, directly or indirectly, for any reason whatever, in the internal or external affairs of any other State. Consequently, armed intervention and all other forms of interference or attempted threats against the personality of the State or against its political, economic and cultural elements, are in violation of international law... No State may use or encourage the use of economic, political or any other type of measures to coerce another State in order to obtain from it the subordination of the exercise of its sovereign rights and to secure from it advantages of any kind....

The same clear prohibition, which emanates from the Charter of the United Nations and is universally acknowledged to have attained the status of binding international law, has been repeated and reaffirmed in numerous other resolutions of the General Assembly, and in other international instruments such as, for example, the Vienna Convention on the Law of Treaties and the Charter of the OAS.

The new measure imposed by the United States violates the rights of third countries to determine their own "external affairs." By disrupting existing shipping routes and increasing the costs of trade with Cuba, the United States attempts — as it frankly concedes — to coerce third countries into abandoning their sovereign decision to maintain normal trade relations with another country.

The new measure is similarly meant to coerce Cuba's sovereign will with respect to its "internal" affairs. It cannot be doubted that the intensity and comprehensive character of the United States embargo, now augmented by this new measure, amounts to economic coercion. Nor can it be doubted from the historical record or from the United States unabashed explanations for continuing its blockade today that the purpose of this unparalleled economic coercion against Cuba is "the subordination of the exercise of its sovereign rights and to secure from its advantages."

The United States measures are also in flagrant disregard of the principles of free trade and commerce reaffirmed many times by the General Assembly and set forth definitively in the Charter of Economic Rights and Duties of States (resolution 3281 [XXIX]), which provides in relevant part:

> Article 4: Every State has the right to engage in international trade and other forms of economic cooperation irrespective of any differences in political, economic and social systems. No State shall be subjected to discrimination of any kind based solely on such differences....

This provision, as others in the Charter of Economic Rights and Duties of States, applies to the field of international economic relations the fundamental principles of sovereign equality of States, non-intervention and the duty to cooperate, which are the bedrock of the Charter of the United Nations and of international law. It is noteworthy that, while some member

States may have expressed reservations with respect to this or other provisions of the Charter of Economic Rights and Duties of States on a variety of grounds, they have nonetheless expressed through the European Community's above-quoted communication their objection to the United States most recent measure, so extreme and unjustified is its interference with their sovereign decision to maintain normal trade and shipping relations with Cuba.

Moreover, the United States measures patently violate both the rights of third countries and of Cuba to free trade and shipping guaranteed by the General Agreement on Tariffs and Trade, which is fully binding on the United States. Article V of the General Agreement on Tariffs and Trade (GATT) recognizes "the freedom of transit through the territory of each contracting party, via the routes most convenient for international transit" of goods, vessels and other means of transport "to or from the territory of other contracting parties." This right of free transit applies irrespective of the "place of origin, departure, entry, exit or destination, or on any circumstances relating to the ownership of [the] goods." The United States refusal, therefore, to permit third-country vessels to enter United States ports because they are carrying cargo in transit to or from Cuba derogates in the starkest terms from its obligations to the international community under Article V.

The right of free transit codified in Article V, moreover, has long been recognized as an essential element in the international protection of commerce. As long ago as 1921, the Convention and Statute on Freedom of Transit (the "Barcelona Convention"), upon which Article V of GATT was based, required States to permit free transit by rail or waterway for international commerce. The Permanent Court of International Justice affirmed the right of free transit recognized in the Barcelona Convention in its decision in *The Railway Traffic Between Lithuania and Poland Case* (Ser. A/B, No. 42, pp. 108, 120 and 121 [1931]).

The executive order is likewise contrary to fundamental treaty obligations because, in violation of Article XI of GATT, it imposes impermissible restrictions upon the importation into the United States of goods from third countries with which the United States has no dispute. Article XI expressly forbids any "prohibitions or restrictions other than duties, taxes or other charges" upon the importation of a product of another contracting State. Yet the United States has imposed a restriction not authorized by Article XI, namely, that the imported goods not be shipped to the United States aboard vessels that are also carrying cargo in transit to or from Cuba.

There can be no justification for the United States violation of these treaty rights of transit and commerce. Article XXI relieves a contracting party from its obligations under GATT only to the extent necessary for the "protection of its essential security interests... in time of war or other emergency in international relations." As noted, the United States no longer even pretends that Cuba threatens its security interests, and the only emergency in international relations is that posed by the United States continuing efforts to intervene in Cuba's internal affairs and deny the rights of third countries to determine their own relations with Cuba.

Thus, this newest measure serves to confirm our prior contention that the United States blockade violates the most basic principles of the United Nations and of international law, and merits the condemnation of the General Assembly.

Talking points

The European Community has made its position clear: Washington should stay out of the trade affairs of other nations. The EC has repeatedly protested both the Mack Amendment and the Torricelli Act, specifically as they attempt to make into law the extraterritorial nature of the embargo. Following are the EC's "Talking Points" distributed on Capitol Hill in June 1992; the Démarche of April 7, 1992; and the Démarche of October 21, 1991.

TALKING POINTS
June 1992

We have commented on a number of occasions about the extraterritorial use of U.S. law with respect to Cuba. Démarches to the Department of State were made on April 7, 1992, October 21, 1991, and letters sent to Congress on September 6 and February 14, 1991.

The U.S. Administration has signalled to Congress its support for the passage of a Cuban Democracy Act, most recently in a letter from the president to Congressman Broomfield, the Ranking Minority Member of the Committee on Foreign Affairs of the House of Representatives. The draft legislation which has passed the House Foreign Affairs Committee contains two provisions to which we object. These are:

— The Mack amendment, which would deny licenses under the Cuban Assets Control Regime to U.S. subsidiaries located outside the U.S. which are owned or controlled by U.S. parent companies;

— A provision which would effectively prohibit any vessel, which had entered Cuba to engage in trade, from visiting U.S. ports for 180 days after departure from Cuba, irrespective of the cargo on board.

This latter measure would reinforce new regulations promulgated by the Treasury Department in April 1992 which will have the effect of prohibiting the entry of any vessel into a U.S. port if the vessel is carrying goods or passengers to or from Cuba or carrying goods in which Cuba or a Cuban national has an interest.

These regulations are in conflict with long-standing rules on comity and international shipping and will adversely affect the European Community's trade with the United States. Since the prohibition on the entry of vessels will not seemingly apply to specifically licensed foreign subsidiary trade, the regulations could also have a discriminatory effect in favor of U.S.-owned or controlled firms located abroad which, regarding their licensed trade with Cuba, would not be subject to shipping restrictions.

We are concerned at the apparent willingness of the U.S. government to endorse passage of a Cuban Democracy Act containing extraterritorial elements which will disrupt the normal business activities of companies and shipping lines based in Member States of the European Community. These measures would constitute the second batch of actions (following the Treasury regulations referred to above) which would be aimed at forcing foreign persons outside the proper jurisdiction of the United States to submit to U.S. law and foreign policy.

As we have reiterated on countless occasions, such extraterritorial extension of U.S. jurisdiction is unacceptable as a matter of law and policy. It is also in outright contradiction with the view frequently expressed by the U.S. government, most notably in the framework of the EC-1992 program, that U.S. enterprises domiciled in foreign countries should benefit from national treatment. Forcing such enterprises to submit to U.S. law denies them the national treatment that the United States espouses for them in other contexts.

We hope that the U.S. Administration and Congress will reflect further on the expediency of supporting legislation which has the capacity to cause damage to trade relations at a time when the bilateral and multilateral agenda is already overcharged. Recognition by allied countries of different economic and foreign policy approaches to countries should be a normal result of international discourse between them. Attempts to force one country's agenda on the other can only lead to conflict and to a denial of the principles that the EC-U.S. Transatlantic

Declaration is designed to underpin.

DEMARCHE FROM THE EUROPEAN COMMUNITY TO THE UNITED STATES STATE DEPARTMENT
April 7, 1992

The Delegation of the Commission of the European Communities and the Embassy of Portugal present their compliments to the Department of State and wish to refer to HR. 4168, the Cuban Democracy Act of 1992, which was recently introduced in the House by Representative Torricelli (D-NJ) and others.

The European Community and its Member States are seriously concerned about Section 6 of the bill which would have the effect of prohibiting U.S.-owned or controlled subsidiary companies domiciled outside the United States from trading with Cuba.

As has been made clear to the Department of State on a number of occasions, most recently in a démarche of October 21, 1991, the European Community and its Member States cannot accept the extraterritorial extension of U.S. jurisdiction as a matter of law and policy.

In addition, the European Community and its Member States note with concern that the bill would introduce discriminatory tax penalties against U.S. companies with subsidiaries overseas which trade with Cuba, thereby providing a draconian economic disincentive against transactions which would be permitted in other jurisdictions.

The bill, if adopted, would also prohibit any vessel from engaging in trade with the United States if the vessel has entered a port in Cuba during the preceding 180 days. Such a measure would be in conflict with long-standing rules on comity and international law, would injure international shipping and would adversely affect the European Community's trade with the United States.

The European Community and its Member States consider that these collective provisions have the potential to cause grave and damaging effects to bilateral EC/U.S. trade relations. Furthermore, passage of these provisions would be totally inappropriate and inconsistent with the new climate of reinforced transatlantic cooperation.

The European Community and its Member States request therefore that the Administration take measures to prevent the bill from passing into law.

The Embassies of Sweden and Canada associate themselves with this démarche.

The Delegation of the Commission of the European Communities and the Embassy of Portugal avail themselves of this opportunity to renew to the Department of State the assurance of their highest consideration.

DEMARCHE OF THE EUROPEAN COMMUNITY
October 21, 1991

The Delegation of the Commission of the European Communities and the Embassy of Ireland present their compliments to the Department of State and wish to refer to the Smith Amendment incorporated in Bill HR 4445, entitled "The Emerging Democracies Act of 1990," as well as to similar language included in Bill S. 2444 introduced in the Senate by Senator Mack and others.

The amendment and the bill contain these objectionable elements:

They would invariably lead to conflicts and arguments over the extraterritorial application of U.S. laws. The European Community and its Member States have repeatedly expressed their concerns on extraterritorial requirements attached to U.S. foreign policy measures. The amendment and the bill would also have a significant impact on the trade interests of the Community and may create conflicting legal requirements for non-U.S. companies to the extent that they may violate U.S. law while acting in perfect conformity with the law of the country in which they are incorporated.

As regards the proposed prohibition on certain transactions between subsidiaries of U.S. firms incorporated outside the USA and Cuba, the bills would have the effect of repealing Section 515.559 (Title 31) of the Code of Federal Regulations, which provides for the issue of licenses to allow so-called U.S.-owned or controlled firms in third countries to do business with Cuba. The European Community would like to recall the Démarche presented to the Department of State on September 15, 1989 in relation to that same Amendment to the Senate version of the Foreign Relations Authorization Bill (repealing Section 515.599), since the Community is still of the view that the United States has no basis in international law to claim the right to license non-U.S. transactions with Cuba by companies incorporated outside the USA, whatever their ownership or control.

As regards the proposed seizure, forfeiture, and sale by the United States of vessels which entered Cuban ports and subsequently U.S. ports, the European Community considers that measure, which even in war time would be an infringement of international law on neutral shipping, is completely unacceptable in peace time.

In addition, the amendment contains measures to withhold assistance from countries importing sugar from Cuba. The European Community considers this a measure with potentially damaging and disturbing effects on international relations for a number of third countries, including from the European Community and some of the states in which both the United States and the European Community and its Member States give aid within the framework of the G-14 process.

The European Community and its Member States therefore urge the Department of State to do all that it can to prevent the enacting of Bill HR 4445 in its current version and of Bill S 2444.

Cuba's draft resolution to the United Nations General Assembly
November 11, 1991

Necessity of ending the economic, commercial and financial embargo imposed by the United States of America against Cuba

The General Assembly

Reaffirming the purpose of the United Nations to develop friendly relations among nations based on respect for the principle of equal rights and self-determination of peoples, and to take other appropriate measures to strengthen universal peace,

Recalling its resolution 2131 (XX) of December 21, 1965, the annex to which contains the Declaration on the Inadmissibility of Intervention in the Domestic Affairs of States and the Protection of Their Independence and Sovereignty, which establishes, inter alia, that no State may use or encourage the use of economic, political or any other type of measures to coerce another State in order to obtain from it the subordination of the exercise of its sovereign rights,

Recalling also its resolution 2625 (XXV) of October 24, 1970, the annex to which contains the Declaration on the Principles of International Law concerning Friendly Relations and Cooperation among States in accordance with the Charter of the United Nations, which reaffirms, inter alia, the duty of States to refrain in their international relations from military, political, economic or any other form of coercion aimed against the political independence or territorial integrity of any State,

Recalling further its resolution 36/103 of December 9, 1981, the annex to which contains the Declaration on the Inadmissibility of Intervention and Interference in the Internal Affairs of States, which sets forth, inter alia, the duty of a State, in the conduct of its international relations, to refrain from measures which would constitute interference or intervention in the internal or external affairs of another State, including any multilateral or unilateral economic reprisal or blockade, as instruments of political pressure or coercion against another State, in violation of the Charter of the United Nations,

Considering that for more than 30 years, a series of economic, commercial and financial measures and actions has been applied against Cuba, causing serious harm to the Cuban people and infringing the sovereignty of that country,

Considering, in particular, that the implementation of those measures and actions is being extraterritorially extended, constituting a blockade against Cuba which not only affects the normal development of international relations but also impairs the inalienable right of the affected countries to exercise freely the prerogatives deriving from their national sovereignty,

Reaffirming the right of every country freely to choose its economic, commercial and financial partners, in exercise of its national sovereignty, without any constraint or interference,

1. Declares that that policy contradicts the principles embodied in the Charter of the United Nations and in international law;

2. Affirms the necessity of ending that policy and, to that effect, calls for an immediate end to the measures and actions comprising it;

3. Invites the international community to extend to Cuba the necessary cooperation to mitigate the consequences of that policy;

4. Requests the Secretary-General to report to the General Assembly at its 47th session on the implementation of the present resolution;

5. Decides to include the item entitled "Necessity of ending the economic, commercial and financial embargo imposed by the United States of America against Cuba" in the provisional agenda of the 47th session of the General Assembly.

Also from Ocean Press

The Cuban Revolution and the United States: A Chronological History

by Jane Franklin

An invaluable resource for scholars, teachers, journalists, legislators, and anyone interested in international relations, this volume offers an unprecedented vision of Cuba-U.S. relations. Cuba watchers will wonder how they got along without it.

Based on exceptionally wide research, this history provides a day by day, year by year report of developments involving Cuba and the United States from January 1959, through to 1990. An introductory section, starting with the arrival of Christopher Columbus in the Caribbean, chronicles the events that led to the triumph of the revolution in Cuba in 1959.

Indispensable as a reference guide, *The Cuban Revolution and the United States* is also an eye-opening narrative, interrelating major crises with seemingly minor or secretive episodes.

Introduction by Louis A. Pérez, Jr.

Published in association with the Center for Cuban Studies

276pp, photos, glossary, index

ISBN paper 1-875284-26-5